Lighted Windows

The Bible Reading Fellowship
15 The Chambers, Vineyard
Abingdon OX14 3FE
brf.org.uk

The Bible Reading Fellowship (BRF) is a Registered Charity (233280)

ISBN 978 0 85746 432 3
First published 2002
This edition 2016
10 9 8 7 6 5 4 3 2 1 0
All rights reserved

Acknowledgements
Unless otherwise stated, scripture quotations are taken from The New Revised Standard Version
of the Bible, Anglicised edition, copyright © 1989, 1995 by the Division of Christian Education
of the National Council of the Churches of Christ in the United States of America. Used by
permission. All rights reserved.

Scripture quotations taken from The Jerusalem Bible © 1966, 1967, 1968 by Darton, Longman
& Todd Ltd and Doubleday & Company, Inc.

Every effort has been made to trace and contact copyright owners for material used in this
resource. We apologise for any inadvertent omissions or errors, and would ask those concerned
to contact us so that full acknowledgement can be made in the future.

A catalogue record for this book is available from the British Library

Printed and bound by CPI Group (UK) Ltd, Croydon CR0 4YY

Lighted Windows

An Advent calendar
for a world in waiting

MARGARET SILF

Preface

It was a dark December night. I was driving through northern Europe on a pre-Christmas visit to friends. The journey was tedious, along endless kilometres of motorway, with little to relieve the monotony. In the intense darkness between built-up areas there seemed to be nothing to hold on to. Then I caught sight of a solitary Christmas tree on the roadside in the middle of nowhere, its lights twinkling bravely against the backdrop of a cold dark night. A delightful surprise! Yet my reaction was a bit ambivalent. On the one hand the tree spoke of courage and resilience, defying the darkness with the determined glow of its tiny lights. On the other hand, its very existence seemed so futile. What difference could a few little lights make to such a dark night? Perhaps it all depended on where I focused my attention—on the lights or on the darkness.

Many years ago, in 2002, *Lighted Windows* saw the light of day for the first time. A great deal has happened since then. In some ways the world has been turned upside down by immense changes that none of us could then have imagined. Much of that change has been challenging and sometimes terrifying, as the human family has faced the first clear manifestations of climate change, the faltering of many of our financial, political and religious institutions, and the impact of savage and indiscriminate brutality. Where are our lighted windows now? Will the lights on the tree of humanity prevail, or the surrounding darkness? Faith says 'yes' to the power of the light. Faith trusts that when the full story is told, light and life will ultimately prevail over darkness and death.

A person of faith is one who desires to live this level of trust in practice. It isn't easy. It is risky and counter-intuitive.

As I write, the first daffodils are coming into bloom. In the neighbourhood gardens the snowdrops and crocuses have been showing their colours for several weeks now. And the date? The third week in January! These flowers are living the risk of faith, pitching vulnerability against hope. While I rejoice in this premature springtime abundance, brought about by an unusually mild winter, my common sense tells me that this is not wise; that there may be many winter storms still to face. Should I rejoice over the January daffodils or bewail their fragility and unpreparedness for what might still lie ahead, their apparent helplessness in the face of unforeseeable situations?

There is a saying that 'faith is like the bird that feels the light and sings before the dawn' (Rabindrath Tagore, 1861–1941). And there are indeed birds who sing their solitary songs about half an hour before the regular dawn chorus begins. If we ask what it might mean to live our faith in a dark world and not to lose heart, perhaps the January daffodils, the lonely Christmas tree and the bird who greets the light before it actually arrives can help and encourage us. *Lighted Windows* is written in this spirit. It invites you to trust the light of your own small candle in a world that can feel hostile and forbidding, and to notice the many other lights that await you along the way, if you have eyes to see, and if you refuse to let your heart focus only on the darkness. It invites you to look beyond your own feelings of helplessness in the face of world situations, and trust in an unseen, yet foundational goodness holding all in being.

At Christmas we remember that a newborn child in a makeshift shelter has become the most potent proof of an indestructible strength that lies in the heart of our human fragility. Today helpless children are camping on our own borders. Migrant families fleeing violence and terror arrive on our own shores every day. How can we light up a window in the heart of the world's desperation today? If God-with-us is the reality that our faith affirms, that reality must be born again and again, in our own time and our own place, and in ways we might prefer to ignore. The seasons of Advent and Christmas remind us that *now* is the time and *ours* is the place in which God is labouring to come to birth.

May your own Advent journey, and your life's journey, be guided by unexpected lights along the roadside that refuse to be extinguished. May it be accompanied by melodies celebrating that which has not yet arrived. And may we ourselves become bearers of a Spirit-kindled light in a world that longs, like never before, for hope and trust and a reason to believe in the best that humanity can become.

Contents

Introduction

Lighted Windows

The First of December, and Christmas is just around the corner! It's the season of expectation, of hope, of anticipation. A season of dreams, and, for Christians, a season where the deepest dream of all humankind meets, face to face, with God's own dream for God's creation, made visible and tangible to everyone who seeks.

One of my most abiding memories is of an evening shared with a friend who had experienced a particularly traumatic childhood. We were talking about our favourite fairy stories, and she told me, with tears in her eyes, of how much the story of 'The Little Match-girl' had come to mean for her, not just in her dreams but in her Christian journeying too.

'The Little Match-girl' wasn't a story I was familiar with, but as she retold it, it came to life in a way that reflects, for me, something of the spirit of this Advent journey. The little match-girl was a young child, undernourished and very poor. She earned her daily bread by selling matches, but the earnings were sparse, and at home a cruel father was waiting to punish her if she failed to bring home enough money. One dark winter night she was standing in her usual place, shivering, and gazing at the lighted windows of the big houses all around her, catching fleeting glimpses of all that was going on inside those rooms—the preparations for

Christmas, the lovely gifts, the bright decorations, the happy faces, the smell of Christmas puddings and roasting goose.

All she had was a box of matches, and there were no customers tonight—they all had other things on their minds. 'Dare I strike one?' she wondered. She took out a match, and struck it, gazing for a few brief moments into its blaze of light. As she did so, she imagined that it was one of those lighted windows. She looked inside, in her imagination, and entered into a warm room where loving friends might welcome her. Another match; another scene. Another window to look into. Perhaps a fine dinner set out for a family. The crackling of the goose, the aroma of mince pies. Food and shelter. And so she continued, until she came to the last match in the box.

The story has a bittersweet ending. As she strikes her last match, the little match-girl sees a shooting star falling across the night sky, and her granny is standing there, smiling, waiting to gather the child into her arms and carry her home to heaven. The frozen child is discovered the next morning, with an empty matchbox in her hands and a deep, contented smile across her white face.

This Advent journey invites you to share something of the magic and the mystery of what it means to look into some of your own 'lighted windows'. But these are not the windows of fantasy. They are the windows of our common quest to discover 'God-with-us'—Emmanuel, God incarnate in the world of everyday reality with all its shame and its glory. They are like the 'windows' of an Advent Calendar, leading us ever closer to the mystery that is born in Bethlehem.

During the first three weeks of the journey, we look, day by day, into a series of windows opening up into glimpses of how we might discover God's guidance in our lives, how we might become more trusting of that guidance, and how we might catch something of God's wisdom.

During Christmas week, the 'windows' open wide, inviting us to enter right into the heart of the mystery of God's coming to earth.

And as the journey moves on through to the turning of the year, and the feast of the Epiphany, the windows turn into doors, through which we are sent out again into a world that is waiting—and longing—for the touch of God's love upon its broken heart.

The child who comes to us in Bethlehem is also cradled in bitter sweetness, like the child in the story. The starlight will turn into the interrogator's beam; the straw will become a crown of thorns. Yet this will be the eye of the needle that will open into a wholeness and completeness that our earthbound hearts and minds cannot begin to imagine.

Each day's reflection includes an invitation to look into its 'window' in a way that connects the God-story with *your* story and *your* circumstances, in a personal way—a way that makes a difference—so that God-with-us becomes ever more authentically God-with-*you*.

May your journey be blessed and joyful, and may it lead you daily more deeply into who you truly are—the person God dreamed you to be when God created you.

1–7 December

Glimpses of Guidance

Most of us find ourselves wishing from time to time that 'someone would show us the way'. During the next few days we look at some of the ways in which guidance is given and how we react to it.

We begin and end this part of the Advent journey with John the Baptist—a man who allowed God to guide him, and who became a guide to others. As the days go by, we pause to reflect on how God's guidance is to be found in:

- The call to take risks (1 December)
- The tendency of God to break right through our careful planning (2 December)
- The touch of God when we are in the pits of despair (3 December)
- The leading of God through our life's mazes (4 December)
- The challenge to go beyond set 'answers' (5 December)
- The choices we make, moment by moment (6 December)
- The signposts we discover, that point beyond themselves to God (7 December)

1 December

Risks

Then there appeared to [Zechariah] an angel of the Lord, standing at the right side of the altar of incense. When Zechariah saw him, he was terrified; and fear overwhelmed him. But the angel said to him, 'Do not be afraid, Zechariah, for your prayer has been heard. Your wife Elizabeth will bear you a son and you will name him John... He will turn many of the people of Israel to the Lord their God...'

Zechariah said to the angel, 'How will I know that this is so? For I am an old man and my wife is getting on in years.' The angel replied, 'I am Gabriel. I stand in the presence of God, and I have been sent to speak to you and to bring you this good news. But now, because you did not believe my words, which will be fulfilled in their time, you will become mute, unable to speak, until the day these things occur.'

...When his time of service was ended, he went to his home.

After those days his wife Elizabeth conceived...

Now the time came for Elizabeth to give birth, and she bore a son. Her neighbours and relatives heard that the Lord had shown his great mercy to her, and they rejoiced with her.

On the eighth day they came to circumcise the child, and they were going to name him Zechariah after his father. But his mother said, 'No; he is to be called John.' They said to her, 'None of your relatives has this name.' Then they began motioning to his father to find out what name he wanted to give him. He asked for a writing-tablet and wrote, 'His name is John.' And all of them were amazed. Immediately his mouth was opened and his tongue freed, and he began to speak, praising God.

LUKE 1:11–24, 57–64 (ABRIDGED)

'If only God would write divine instructions across the sky,' we might often be tempted to think. If only it were obvious what we should do, which direction we should choose, how we should react to a particular person or situation. But life rarely gives us that kind of certainty. More often our choices and decisions are full of ambiguity and mixed motivation, and the best we can hope for is to do a minimum of harm—a goal so far removed from the desire that burns in our hearts to live true to the very best of our visions.

Perhaps, as the years go by, our attempts to follow the path of God, however we envision it, may become like Zechariah's—refined, but also reduced, to the faithful fulfilment of a set of obligations and the leading of what might pass as 'a good life'. Such faithfulness is never to be despised. It can be the seedbed of God's kingdom. Unfortunately, it can all too easily turn into a comfort zone. We feel so settled in our holy niche that we stop even expecting God to intervene in our lives. We carry on 'burning our incense'. We keep on tending that flickering little fire within us that still burns with a love for God. But we don't expect to wake up one morning and discover that the flames are suddenly leaping out of control. Neither did Zechariah!

In short, our waiting upon God can become simply the habit of waiting, for its own sake—like waiting day on day in line at the bus-stop, but being wholly unprepared for the possibility that the bus might actually arrive. So stunned are we when the bus turns up that we step back in disbelief, and refuse to get on board. How do we know that the bus isn't some figment of our imagination? How do we know that this is really 'our' bus, and will take us to where we want to be? What if we can't pay the fare? What if it all turns out to be too costly? Maybe it would be just so much easier, and safer, to stay in line at the bus-stop. After all, we know where we are when we're standing at the bus-stop. Who knows where we might end up if we get on the bus?

We might imagine Zechariah going through a process of thought a bit like this. His faithful lifelong prayers for God's guidance are suddenly answered, and he doesn't know how to respond. His coping mechanism is to try to interpret the divine touch of God in terms of merely human logic: 'This doesn't make sense within my terms of reference, so I will dismiss it.' But God's touch, as we know from our own experience, confounds human logic and goes far beyond it. Often, the best, most visionary things we do in life are fuelled not by reason and logic but by intuition, imagination and desire.

Zechariah's story encourages me. It reminds me that I'm not the only one to fail to recognise God's guidance even when it is given to me on a plate, and that however stubbornly I fail to respond, God's purposes will not be deflected on that account. Elizabeth's child is going to come into the world, whatever his father may think about the possibility. It is Zechariah, and not God, who is disempowered by his refusal to respond to the guidance he is being given.

I am encouraged too by the fact that the disempowerment was not permanent. Just as the infant John would need nine months' gestation before coming to birth, so Zechariah is also given a time of gestation in which his response can grow and ripen into the whole-hearted 'Yes' expressed in the moment when he writes on the tablet, 'His name is John.'

God will wait for our response and will wait for as long as it takes.

'How will I know that this is so?'

When you got up this morning, you had no idea what the day would bring. But you probably chose to take a chance on it, and not go back to bed. God invites us to take a chance on life too, without knowing where God's guidance will lead us. To the extent that we can say 'Yes', we will discover the next step along the way. To the extent that we hold back, we will get stuck where we are, until we are ready to move on again. How do you feel about the response you want to make to God in the light of the challenges today will bring?

Lord, I can't see the bright sunlight of your leading, because my eyes are focused on the little candle of my own thinking. Blow out the candle if you must, and give me the grace to see your light in my darkness. Amen

Plans

Moses was keeping the flock of his father-in-law Jethro, the priest of Midian; he led his flock beyond the wilderness, and came to Horeb, the mountain of God. There the angel of the Lord appeared to him in a flame of fire out of a bush; he looked, and the bush was blazing, yet it was not consumed. Then Moses said, 'I must turn aside and look at this great sight, and see why the bush is not burned up.' When the Lord saw that he had turned aside to see, God called to him out of the bush, 'Moses, Moses!' And he said, 'Here I am.' Then he said, 'Come no closer! Remove the sandals from your feet, for the place on which you are standing is holy ground.' He said further, 'I am the God of your father, the God of Abraham, the God of Isaac, and the God of Jacob.' And Moses hid his face, for he was afraid to look at God.

Then the Lord said, 'I have observed the misery of my people who are in Egypt; I have heard their cry on account of their taskmasters. Indeed, I know their sufferings… The cry of the Israelites has now come to me; I have also seen how the Egyptians oppress them. So come, I will send you to Pharaoh to bring my people, the Israelites, out of Egypt.' But Moses said to God, 'Who am I that I should go to Pharaoh, and bring the Israelites out of Egypt?' He said, 'I will be with you; and this shall be the sign for you that it is I who sent you: when you have brought the people out of Egypt, you shall worship God on this mountain.'

EXODUS 3:1–12 (ABRIDGED)

I wonder how many years of my life I have actually spent 'waiting'. I don't mean just those hours waiting in queues or in traffic jams, or on one end of multiple-choice telephone lines with no sign of a human being at the other. At times like that, the 'waiting game' is an obvious frustration. No, I am thinking more of all those days I have spent staring out of the office window or at the view from the kitchen sink, thinking to myself that everything will be better when such-and-such happens. With this kind of mindset, I have spent literally years and years waiting—waiting for the holidays to come round, for the boss to move on, for the next promotion or the next exam, waiting for children to arrive, waiting for them to grow up and be independent and then waiting for them to come home again to visit! The grass is quite simply *always* going to be greener around the next bend in the road.

The same kind of logic has shaped my search for God's guidance in my life. I have sat down in prayer, and set out my plans, pointing out, in ways God surely couldn't misunderstand, exactly where I needed help. And then I have been unpleasantly surprised when that guidance wasn't, apparently, forthcoming.

Maybe Moses was prey to thoughts like these, too, as he tended his father-in-law's flocks at Horeb. He had been forced to flee from justice, having killed an Egyptian who was harassing one of the Israelites—a change of plan that he had probably not bargained for. And we find him now looking after the sheep, biding his time, and keeping a low profile.

God has other plans. Into the midst of Moses' neat arrangements comes a burning bush! Suddenly he is confronted by something wholly unexpected. Thankfully, for all of us, Moses had enough space in his heart and mind to give God a chance to break through. He had the grace to see the burning bush and to take it seriously. He was willing to put his own planning on hold and, as it were, switch channels, to listen to what God was trying to communicate.

What can we learn from this encounter about the pattern of God's guidance? A few thoughts come to mind:

- God's guidance attracts us, it doesn't coerce us.
- It usually takes us by surprise.
- It happens when we are going about our everyday living, and it grows out of that everyday experience, if we have eyes to see.
- It is not destructive, although it sometimes seems as if it will be. We have to cross a threshold of trust if we want to engage with it.
- We have to come close enough to hear it.
- We will recognise it in those moments when we sense that we are on holy ground.
- It may lead us to where we would rather not go.

God's guidance may begin with a peak experience for ourselves, but it is given for the benefit of more than just ourselves. Our God is a relational God—a trinity of Father, Son and Spirit—and the guidance God gives is not just for ourselves, but to be put into practice in a relational, interdependent world.

'The place on which you are standing is holy ground'

Perhaps you can look back on moments that have shaped or reshaped your life. It might be helpful to reflect on these experiences in the light of Moses' encounter with the burning bush. How did you react when you felt God's touch on your life in some powerful way? What guidance was given? How did it tally with your own 'planning'? Was it just for you, or did it have wider implications? How did you work it out in practice? Or perhaps you didn't recognise it at all at the time, but can only see its outworkings with the benefit of hindsight.

An acquaintance of mine, whose life had been recently derailed, once said to me, 'What makes God laugh? Answer: People who make plans!' Let us not become so entangled in the shaping of our years that we miss the signpost that is standing right here in the present moment.

Lord, please help me to laugh, with you, about my own so-serious planning, and then let us move on together in the light of your surprises. Amen

Pits

[Elijah] was afraid; he got up and fled for his life, and came to Beersheba, which belongs to Judah; he left his servant there.

But he himself went a day's journey into the wilderness, and came and sat down under a solitary broom tree. He asked that he might die: 'It is enough; now, O Lord, take away my life, for I am no better than my ancestors.' Then he lay down under the broom tree and fell asleep. Suddenly an angel touched him and said to him, 'Get up and eat.' He looked, and there at his head was a cake baked on hot stones, and a jar of water. He ate and drank, and lay down again. The angel of the Lord came a second time, touched him, and said, 'Get up and eat, otherwise the journey will be too much for you.' He got up, and ate and drank; then he went in the strength of that food forty days and forty nights to Horeb the mount of God. At that place he came to a cave, and spent the night there...

[God] said, 'Go out and stand on the mountain before the Lord, for the Lord is about to pass by.' Now there was a great wind, so strong that it was splitting mountains and breaking rocks in pieces before the Lord, but the Lord was not in the wind; and after the wind an earthquake, but the Lord was not in the earthquake; and after the earthquake a fire, but the Lord was not in the fire; and after the fire a sound of sheer silence. When Elijah heard it, he wrapped his face in his mantle and went out and stood at the entrance of the cave.
1 KINGS 19:3–13 (ABRIDGED)

It's strangely reassuring to know that the mightiest prophets can also suffer from depression and find themselves drawing a complete blank in their attempt to discover what God is up to. This kind of despair seems to bring down the curtains on all our spiritual journeying. It can stop us in our tracks. We lie down and sink into our own personal dark pit. Like an accident victim on a cold, exposed mountainside, all we want to do is to sink into oblivion. The desire to sleep away our sorrows can lead us to a real risk of spiritual hypothermia, the kind of sleep from which we may never awaken.

This seems to be the mood Elijah is in today. He is wishing he were dead, and is telling God how he feels. Perhaps you know the place in your own experience?

So where is God's guidance when we find ourselves at the end of our rope? And what chance of finding it, let alone of following it? Maybe this incident from Elijah's story can give us a few clues, as it reveals how God deals with this kind of despair—a pattern that is just as relevant today as it was in the time of Elijah.

- First, God encourages us to express how we feel. Often a listener appears—someone we can trust—possibly not the person we would have expected or even chosen, but someone, nevertheless, and that someone may be our 'angel'.
- Next, God gives us (through our 'angel') something, maybe a small something, to boost our positive energy a bit, and to stop us falling into the sleep of despair. For Elijah it was simple fare—bread and water—but fresh and appetising and just enough to revive his spirits.
- Then God waits, until we are ready, and, when the right moment comes, gives us a bit more to strengthen us for the onward journey.

When I look back over the ups and downs of my own life (especially the downs), I can see how this pattern has recurred. The intervention that made a difference has come to me through 'angels'. The 'angels' may have been colleagues or neighbours or even complete strangers. At the time, I probably didn't recognise the hand of God in their kindness and their caring, but with hindsight I can see clearly that these were definitive moments that drew me beyond despair, and gave me strength to keep going.

Often such guidance has come gradually, one step at a time, bringing a little more encouragement each time. It isn't a divine jetliner that carries us to the holy mountain, but our own step-by-step response to the angels' encouragement.

But this isn't the end of the waiting. Even at the mountaintop, Elijah is asked to wait, to observe, and to expect the unexpected. In that waiting space God is revealed in ways we don't expect. Not in the spectacular and loud and fear-inspiring, not in the powerful and earth-shaking, but in the stillness of our hearts.

In this secret, holy place, we will know when God is close, and we will 'cover our faces' in awe. And then, only then, will we hear the instructions for the next step.

'An angel touched him'

Elijah's story gives us a map of the terrain we might be in when we are seeking God's guidance in a time of despair. Does it connect at all to your own experience of being in this kind of terrain? Who have *your* angels been? How have they moved you on? What was the 'bread and water' that kept you going? What does the holy mountain mean for *you*? And do these memories help you to move more trustfully into the future?

It doesn't have to be some cataclysmic disaster that pitches us into despair. In fact, it's much more likely to be that thoughtless word, that undeserved criticism, that creeping anxiety—the very stuff of everyday life. And the journey to the holy mountain needn't be a huge pilgrimage. It can be as simple as going aside for ten minutes to a quiet place where we can tell God how we are feeling, just as Elijah did. We can safely leave the rest to God, just as Elijah did.

Out of the depths I call, Lord; in those depths let me meet you.
Amen

Mazes

When Pharaoh let the people go, God did not lead them by way of the land of the Philistines, although that was nearer; for God thought, 'If the people face war, they may change their minds and return to Egypt.' So God led the people by the roundabout way of the wilderness towards the Red Sea. The Israelites went up out of the land of Egypt prepared for battle. And Moses took with him the bones of Joseph who had required a solemn oath of the Israelites, saying, 'God will surely take notice of you, and then you must carry my bones with you from here.'

They set out from Succoth, and camped at Etham, on the edge of the wilderness. The Lord went in front of them in a pillar of cloud by day, to lead them along the way, and in a pillar of fire by night, to give them light, so that they might travel by day and by night. Neither the pillar of cloud by day nor the pillar of fire by night left its place in front of the people...

Whenever the cloud was taken up from the tabernacle, the Israelites would set out on each stage of their journey; but if the cloud was not taken up, then they did not set out until the day that it was taken up. For the cloud of the Lord was on the tabernacle by day, and fire was in the cloud by night, before the eyes of all the house of Israel at each stage of their journey.

EXODUS 13:17–22; 40:36–38

I have a basalt 'labyrinth stone', formed over six hundred million years ago out of the volcanic turmoil that formed the Lleyn Peninsula in Wales. Shaped and smoothed by the sea through all the ages, and now engraved with the symbol of a labyrinth, this stone has become a prayer stone. It reminds me that the search for God almost never leads in a straight line and that it may demand much patient waiting. When I look back over my life so far, I often want to ask God why on earth we didn't take a quicker, easier route through the various obstacles that presented themselves. With hindsight it always looks as though there would have been a more straightforward, less painful and confusing path.

Labyrinths and mazes are a universal human symbol of the search for what matters most. There seems to be a deep human intuition that the convolutions of life are the very places where we do our growing and our learning. They force us to wait for the next step to become clear. They lead us into cul-de-sacs and backwaters, and bring us face to face with our human limitations. They frustrate us and confound our 'wisdom'. Yet they are our path, and there is no other.

Rivers tell us the same kind of story. When they come up to an obstruction, they find a way to flow around it. No doubt, if a river could speak, it too would express its frustration at the many boulders that have blocked its way. But would it also realise how much more of the barren earth has been visited and watered by its stream in the process?

The Israelites could have taken the coastal road, but God had a hidden agenda. The shortest route would also have provided an easy escape route. How easy to run 'back to Egypt' (and to captivity) at the first difficulty, if the road had been straight and obvious. And yes, I too would have run back to base many a time, when faced with problems too hard to solve, if I could have found the way! As it was, I was so embroiled in the twists and turns of my life's journey that the only way forward was to trust in the next step and wait for some kind of clarity to come out of the confusion. And that trusting and waiting, I discover, has been the way God has been guiding me and growing me all along.

It would be a bleak picture indeed if all we had to hope for was a labyrinth of confusion. But there is more in the maze than we might have dared to hope. There is a dream. And there is a fire.

The Israelites, we learn, carried the bones of Joseph with them on their momentous trek through the desert. Why? Perhaps because Joseph was their dreamer, the symbol of their God-dream. So, though we are urged to travel light, we must carry our dream with us, wherever the labyrinth of life may lead us. The dream is our energy for the road. It is our memory of those moments when God has unmistakably touched our lives. It is a sacred space and a still centre in all our confusion. We need to return to it regularly to replenish our resources for the way.

While we carry the dream, God can be trusted to provide the fire. For the Israelites, as so often for ourselves, the fire of God's leading seems to be concealed in a cloud of unknowing. Paradoxically, it is in the place where we are unable to find our own way that God is most powerfully present to us. The fire at the heart of the cloud only becomes visible at night, when we are in the darkest stretches of our life's journey.

'And fire was in the cloud'

My labyrinth stone has had to wait for millions of years to discover what it really is. While it was being hurled around in the throes of volcanic activity, or battered by the force of the sea, it could never have imagined that one day it would become a pebble that would help to lead a human heart closer to God. It teaches me to do my own waiting with an open and expectant heart. What shape is *your* stone taking?

> *I have a dream, Lord, and you are the fire.*
> *Let us risk the maze of being, hand in hand. Amen*

Answer books

For surely I know the plans I have for you, says the Lord, plans for your welfare and not for harm, to give you a future with hope. Then when you call upon me and come and pray to me, I will hear you. When you search for me, you will find me; if you seek me with all your heart, I will let you find me, says the Lord, and I will restore your fortunes and gather you from all the nations and all the places where I have driven you, says the Lord, and I will bring you back to the place from which I sent you into exile...

But this is the covenant that I will make with the house of Israel after those days, says the Lord: I will put my law within them, and I will write it on their hearts; and I will be their God, and they shall be my people. No longer shall they teach one another, or say to each other, 'Know the Lord', for they shall all know me, from the least of them to the greatest, says the Lord; for I will forgive their iniquity, and remember their sin no more.

JEREMIAH 29:11–14; 31:33–34

Perhaps you have heard the story of the schoolboy who dreamed of becoming a mathematician. This same lad also liked to be out on the town in the evenings, and so he often skipped his homework. When this happened, he would hastily throw his exercises together on the bus the next morning by looking at the answers at the end of the book.

One day his teacher took him to one side and told him just one simple truth: 'You will never become a mathematician by looking up the answers to the problems in the back of the book,' he said, 'even though, ironically, those answers will usually be the right ones.'

Perhaps this wisdom is something of what lies behind the game of hide-and-seek that God appears to be playing with us so often. 'Come on,' God urges us, 'come and look for me. Where have I hidden myself today?'

'Is this game God's idea of fun?' we might be forgiven for wondering. Or is it, rather, God's way of teaching our hearts divine meanings and sacred ways? We might almost hear God whispering, very gently, 'You will never become fully the person I created you to be by cribbing life's answers from creeds and doctrines, even though these doctrines may well be right and true. You will only become your true self by working through for yourself the challenges that life presents.'

A daunting prospect! But from Jeremiah's words today we discover that we are not alone in the task. God has promised to plant the holy law deep within our own hearts. So does this mean that we have some kind of 'answer book' inside us, if we only knew how to access it? I think not, much as we might wish it were so! God's answers don't come ready-made. They have to be discovered. And the prophet goes on to give us a clue about this process of discovery.

This 'law' that God has planted in our hearts, it seems, is more like the bond of a personal relationship than the terms of an equation. It is a sense of alignment between our own hearts and the heart of God that will deepen and strengthen every time we use it, so that gradually, step by step, we will learn to recognise when we are acting out of our truest centre, and when we are slipping off-course. The closer we come to this kind of discernment, the less we will need human guides and teachers.

God's guidance is something organic and alive. God plants it in our hearts, and writes it for each of us uniquely, and then gives it growth, until it bears the fruits of God's kingdom. It is a guidance that leads to right relationship—a mutuality of relationship between God and all God's people. It can't be copied from the back of the book. It has to be lived! It is a journey of discovery, not a system of salvation.

Jeremiah gives us two further clues about the nature of this mysterious 'law' in our hearts:

- It reflects the very dynamic of the holy, always to bring good out of bad, better out of good, and best out of better. The dynamic of evil works the other way round, always diminishing our good to mediocre, and our poor to worst. Observing how these contradictory movements are working in us at any particular moment is an important tool for cooperating with God's 'law'.

- It is for all God's people, not just for those who understand the rules of 'discernment'. It flows from God's own presence deep within our hearts, and that presence is often more obvious in those who are not overburdened with their own 'achievements'.

> 'I will put my law within them,
> and I will write it on their hearts'

There is a beautiful story of how, one day, God was talking with the angels about where to hide within creation, so that humankind might not find God too easily but might grow through their searching.

The first angel suggested the depths of the earth as a hiding place. 'No,' said God. 'They will soon learn to dig mines, and they will find me too soon.'

34

'What about hiding on their moon?' the second angel suggested. 'No,' said God. 'It won't be long before they reach the moon with their technology. They will find me too soon.'

It was the third angel who hit on the Great Idea. 'Why don't you hide yourself in their own hearts?' she suggested. 'They'll never think to look there.' So God did just that, and this is why it takes us so long to find God, step by step as we do our living. And that, in turn, is what makes us grow.

You might like to ask God today to draw you a little closer to the secret depths of your own heart, where the secret of the holy is hidden, for you to discover.

Lord, give me the courage to go beyond my ready-made answers and to know you, rather than merely knowing about you. Amen

Choices

Surely, this commandment that I am commanding you today is not too hard for you, nor is it too far away. It is not in heaven, that you should say, 'Who will go up to heaven for us, and get it for us so that we may hear it and observe it?' Neither is it beyond the sea, that you should say, 'Who will cross to the other side of the sea for us, and get it for us so that we may hear it and observe it?' No, the word is very near to you; it is in your mouth and in your heart for you to observe.

See, I have set before you today life and prosperity, death and adversity. If you obey the commandments of the Lord your God that I am commanding you today, by loving the Lord your God, walking in his ways, and observing his commandments, decrees, and ordinances, then you shall live and become numerous, and the Lord your God will bless you in the land that you are entering to possess. But if your heart turns away and you do not hear, but are led astray to bow down to other gods and serve them, I declare to you today that you shall perish; you shall not live long in the land that you are crossing the Jordan to enter and possess. I call heaven and earth to witness against you today that I have set before you life and death, blessings and curses. Choose life...

DEUTERONOMY 30:11–19

Today we discover a little more about this mysterious 'law' that God has written in our own hearts. Do we have to scour the heavens to find it? Do we have to sail beyond the most distant horizons? Do we have to spend our waking moments buried in library books? Do we have to be Martin Luthers or Mother Teresas? Do we have to be ordained, or vowed to the monastic life? Do we even have to be paid-up members of a church?

Apparently not. The search for this 'law', we learn, happens *within* us, in the context of our everyday living, and in the choices we make as we go about our daily life. 'The word,' God tells us, 'is very near you. You will find it reflected in your own words and actions, choices and relationships. The secret is to learn to live by it.'

This is good news and bad news. The good news is that it is open to everyone, regardless of their intelligence or ability, to discover the guiding of God within themselves. The bad news is that this leaves us no excuse for not following it and putting it into practice.

But God doesn't leave us stumbling around in the dark. God goes on to give us these ground rules for living in true alignment with the holy.

- The nature of God is always to lead in the direction of greater fullness of life. This is God's desire for us. We begin to discover our true 'alignment' when this starts to shape our own desiring too.
- However, there are many counter-attractions that claim to be giving us a fuller life but are actually distracting us from the quest of our hearts for God. Some of these imposters are obvious, as they crowd into our living-rooms each night via TV commercials. Others are much more subtle in their approach.

An important aspect of our journeying is to learn to recognise what form these counter-attractions are taking for each of us personally at any given time or in any given situation, and to seek God's help in dealing with them.

We deal with them most effectively by keeping our main

focus at all times on what is most important to us—our quest to live true to God's stirrings within us. The strength of this desire is, ultimately, stronger than all the lesser wants and wishes that might pull us off-course.

God's great desire is that we should choose *life*, and choosing life, we learn, is not a one-off decision, but a moment-by-moment affair, reflected (or denied) in everything we do. Every choice we make, every reaction and response to life's events, has the potential to draw us towards a fuller life or to diminish us into something less than the best.

'Choose life'

What might it mean in practice to choose life? Well, perhaps we need only look again at the way God works. God's way is, as we have seen, always to bring the good out of the less-than-good. So we are choosing life whenever our own living reflects this dynamic too. This may be in major issues, such as working to resolve a matter of conflict in the family or at work, or it may be as simple as offering a word of encouragement or comfort to someone when we could have chosen to pass by in silence.

And how will we know when we are choosing life? How can we tell whether we are 'living true' or not? In the language of our own lives, the words in today's passage might translate into something like this.

- We will feel in tune with ourselves (deep down) when we are following the call to life, in small ways or in large.
- We will feel at odds with ourselves (deep down) when we let ourselves be side-tracked by things that are not leading to the fullness of life.

We need to be aware, however, that our surface feelings, in any given situation, may not be so clear. They may deceive us, just as a tree may be swayed violently in its topmost branches though its root is firmly grounded in the earth.

Perhaps we might carry one crucial question around with us as we move through the events of our living: 'What does the best in me choose?'

> *Lord, in all I do, the big things and the trivial, help me*
> *to stand still for just a moment to ask, 'What does the best*
> *in me choose to do?' Amen*

Signposts

This is the testimony given by John when the Jews sent priests and Levites from Jerusalem to ask him, 'Who are you?' He confessed and did not deny it, but confessed, 'I am not the Messiah.' And they asked him, 'What then? Are you Elijah?' He said, 'I am not.' 'Are you the prophet?' He answered, 'No.' Then they said to him, 'Who are you? Let us have an answer for those who sent us. What do you say about yourself?' He said, 'I am the voice of one crying out in the wilderness, "Make straight the way of the Lord,"' as the prophet Isaiah said...

'I baptise with water. Among you stands one whom you do not know, the one who is coming after me; I am not worthy to untie the thong of his sandal.' ...

The next day he saw Jesus coming toward him and declared, 'Here is the Lamb of God who takes away the sin of the world! This is he of whom I said, "After me comes a man who ranks ahead of me because he was before me." I myself did not know him; but I came baptising with water for this reason, that he might be revealed to Israel.' ...

The next day John again was standing with two of his disciples, and as he watched Jesus walk by, he exclaimed, 'Look, here is the Lamb of God!' The two disciples heard him say this, and they followed Jesus.
JOHN 1:19–37 (ABRIDGED)

Imagine yourself walking along your local high street on a sunny morning. People all around you are going about their business—perhaps setting up their market stalls for the day, taking the children to school, opening up the shops. But in the middle of it all, one person is standing in the middle of the pavement, gazing up to the sky.

Give the scene another five minutes, and no prizes for guessing how the high street looks now! Some people are still getting on with the morning chores, but meanwhile a large crowd has gathered around the stranger on the pavement who is gazing at the sky. Nothing has been spoken. But they all want to know what it is that is so powerfully engaging the attention of this person.

It wouldn't matter now if the person who started it all were simply to walk away. The crowd is no longer interested in that person as such, but in whatever it was that was attracting that person's gaze.

Of course, it would be possible to instigate a scene like this just for the fun of it, staring at nothing at all, then walking away, leaving a fascinated crowd behind you, likewise staring at they-know-not-what. But John the Baptist isn't having a joke. His focus is firmly on the One who is going to have a profound effect on the world and its story from this moment on.

Yet what he actually does, at this moment at least, is not a million miles from the action of our person in the high street. He simply directs the attention of the crowds to something— Someone—beyond themselves. This gives me a very big clue about where I might discover God's guidance: *I find God's guidance in those who point beyond themselves.*

When I look back over the years, I can name several people who have been 'John the Baptist' for me. Without exception they have been people whose faces have been turned to God, and whose hearts have been focused on God, to such an extent that others were bound to notice and be attracted in the same direction. Usually, I suspect, they never realised the power of their witness. They have been people who were so free of any need for personal status and recognition that they could walk away when their task was done, entrusting the rest to God. And they haven't always been in the places where you might expect such people to be.

By contrast, I have also encountered people, and institutions, who appeared to be doing the opposite—pointing always to themselves rather than to the One who is beyond them. John shows us very graphically how to deal with this tendency towards a 'messiah complex' in ourselves and in others. His answer is a simple, honest, straightforward 'No'. 'No, *I'm* not the One you are looking for. I am only pointing in his direction. *I'm* not your destination. I'm just one of the signposts along your way.' There is a danger in listening to those who claim to have 'the answers' in their own right. There is an even greater danger in becoming such a person ourselves.

And when the awaited one actually appears, John readily lets his own disciples move on. He even encourages them to do so. 'Look, *that's* the man you are looking for. Follow *him*.' The Lord is bigger than all our lesser allegiances—even our allegiance to a particular faith tradition.

'Look, here is the lamb of God'

During this first week of our Advent journey we have explored just a few of the ways in which God guides us. But we who are guided are also called, as John was called, to 'prepare the way of the Lord'—to journey on in such a way that we (perhaps unconsciously) provide pointers to those who follow after. We are challenged to live constantly with our inner eyes fixed on God. We are challenged always to point beyond ourselves.

Where have you discovered pointers to God in your personal story? Which way is the finger of your own life pointing?

Lord, please make my own life into a pointer towards you—
but please don't let me realise you are doing it, in case I am
tempted to turn the signpost back towards myself. Amen

8–14 December

Glimpses of Trust

Trust is a gift that we are born with, but very quickly lose as we grow up. Waiting, in the spirit of Advent, asks a special kind of trust that will cooperate with the coming of God-with-us, without knowing the outcome of our waiting or how long that waiting will last.

During the coming few days we explore what it is that helps us to trust. What makes trusting possible in an untrustworthy world? We begin by joining Mary of Nazareth as she is asked to entrust her whole being to the unknown of God's incarnation, and we end with Joseph as he too goes through the trust threshold, guided by a dream. As we move through the days, we explore how trust can grow through:

- Listening to our own personal experience of the touch of God upon our lives (8 December)
- Going deep into the 'tap root' of our lives, to draw on the resources that flow from God, who is at home in the core of our being (9 December)
- Surrender to the certainty that the Creator knows the ways of life better than the creature does (10 December)
- The discovery that life's simplest aspects are more trustworthy than its many complications (11 December)
- Learning to discern the difference between the kind

of power that seeks to control us and may need to be resisted, and the kind of power that transforms us and invites our loving obedience (12 December)

- The call to be adventurers, investing all we have in the onward journey with the Lord (13 December)
- The potential of our intuitive depths to expose the deeper dreaming below our life's nightmares (14 December)

Experience

In the sixth month the angel Gabriel was sent by God to a town in
Galilee called Nazareth, to a virgin engaged to a man whose name
was Joseph, of the house of David. The virgin's name was Mary.
And he came to her and said, 'Greetings, favoured one! The Lord is
with you.' But she was much perplexed by his words and pondered
what sort of greeting this might be. The angel said to her, 'Do not be
afraid, Mary, for you have found favour with God. And now, you will
conceive in your womb and bear a son, and you will name him Jesus.
He will be great, and will be called the Son of the Most High, and the
Lord God will give to him the throne of his ancestor David. He will
reign over the house of Jacob for ever, and of his kingdom there will
be no end.'

Mary said to the angel, 'How can this be, since I am a virgin?' The
angel said to her, 'The Holy Spirit will come upon you, and the power
of the Most High will overshadow you; therefore the child to be born
will be holy; he will be called Son of God. And now, your relative
Elizabeth in her old age has also conceived a son; and this is the
sixth month for her who was said to be barren. For nothing will be
impossible with God.'

Then Mary said, 'Here am I, the servant of the Lord; let it be with
me according to your word.' Then the angel departed from her.
LUKE 1:26–38

I sometimes ask myself what actually keeps me believing in
the Good News. Is it because someone else says it is true?
That might have worked when I was a child, but it certainly
wouldn't have been enough to keep me with it through the

challenges of adult life. Is it because if I don't keep believing, I may miss out on 'eternal life'? No again. Because that would be a faith based on fear, and fear, though it can force us into doing things we don't want or intend to do, can never move our hearts or ignite our vision. When I really get to the heart of what keeps me believing, I discover it is actually something that on the surface appears to be intangible and rather fragile—it is my own personal experience of the times and the ways in which God has touched my life. Sometimes this touch of God has brought healing or comfort when I thought I was at the end of my rope. Sometimes it has given me the strength to stay in a difficult place or the courage to make necessary changes. Sometimes it has momentarily set my soul alight in a flash of joy that has given me energy to keep moving on, trusting that this experience was coming from a bedrock reality far deeper than my own small conscious world.

Mary's encounter with the angel Gabriel is perhaps one such moment of experience, writ large! What made her able to say 'Yes!' to the angel's request? Mary had certainly been brought up in faithful obedience to the Jewish Law, but I find it hard to believe that this *alone* gave her the trust to hand over her future, her reputation, her body, mind and soul to God as she did. And, though the coming of the angel must have summoned up her fears, these fears seem to have been more like an overwhelming sense of awe at a presence that was larger than life, rather than the fear of something that was bringing harm. Fear alone might have elicited a terrified consent from her, but it would never have kept her faithful through all that was to come.

What seems to have set Mary's soul on fire that morning was surely her own, personal, direct *experience* of the presence of God, granted to her through the vision of the angel. This was so overwhelming, so joy-filled, such an eternal moment, that she would never again doubt the power and the ever-presence of the God from whom it came. 'Yes!' was the only possible response to such an experience.

I find it strangely consoling, too, to learn that Mary immediately *questioned* her own experience. Most of us can identify with her questioning. One moment we can feel God's touch upon our life, the next moment we find ourselves saying, 'This can't be true, because it doesn't fit within my familiar parameters!' The angel counters this questioning not with simple black-and-white answers, but with an assurance that God's ways are infinitely larger than our minds and hearts can ever encompass. Our own rules and patterns can never contain God's transforming power. All we can do—all we are asked to do—is to allow that transforming power to be 'earthed' in our own living. 'Nothing is impossible to God!' All our mindsets are just matchbox-size when it comes to holding the immensity and the potential of God.

Yet this power is not threatening. The angel's first word to Mary is 'Rejoice!', rapidly followed by the assurance that there is nothing to fear. In the light of all that is to come, this might sound like unwarranted optimism. Have we really nothing to fear, if we say our own 'Yes!' to God? Perhaps, again, it is a question of the size of our mindset. To our 'matchbox' thinking, there may well be challenges along the way ahead that will give rise to fear. But the angel's promise is that the overwhelming love of God will always be infinitely stronger than the pull of all our fears. We are not promised an easy 'happy ever after'. What we *are* promised is that the joy we experience when God touches our hearts is the real thing, and nothing else that can happen to us, however difficult or frightening, will ever have more power than that touch. The way of God always leads to new life.

'Let it be with me according to your word'

In the days ahead, we reflect on what it means to wait for God's coming with trust in our hearts. Mary reveals that the basis for this trust is to be found in our own experience. Take a little time to remember those moments in your own life when God has seemed to be especially close. How did you feel then? What was your response? What difference did your experience make to your ongoing journey through life?

Lord, please keep my own heart's 'Yes!' alive through all the questions that may follow. Bring to birth in my life what you conceived in me when your life touched mine. Be with me in all the labour pains that may come, until together we rejoice over the 'You' you have fathered in me. Amen

Depth

Thus says the Lord:
Cursed are those who trust in mere mortals
and make mere flesh their strength,
whose hearts turn away from the Lord.
They shall be like a shrub in the desert,
and shall not see when relief comes.
They shall live in the parched places of the wilderness,
in an uninhabited salt land.

Blessed are those who trust in the Lord,
whose trust is the Lord.
They shall be like a tree planted by water,
sending out its roots by the stream.
It shall not fear when heat comes,
and its leaves shall stay green;
in the year of drought it is not anxious,
and it does not cease to bear fruit.
JEREMIAH 17:5–8

It doesn't take a degree in biology to understand that a plant has the best chance of staying alive if its roots can reach deep sources of water and nourishment. The plant that relies only on its flowers and leaves to keep it going is unlikely to survive the hard times. When the going gets tough, living things return to their deeper sources for the means to survive, whether the threat is from the droughts of summer or the frosts of winter. They return to a root that is deeper than anything we can see at ground level. Perhaps we can learn from them something of what we ourselves need, if our trust in God's companionship and action in our lives is to survive the obstacles it will undoubtedly encounter.

When I look out of the window and see the spreading oak tree outside, its branches help me to return to this 'deeper root'. Sometimes, in prayer and in my daily living, I find myself astride the horns of a dilemma: 'If I do this, I can't do that' or 'If this is the right course, the other course must be wrong.' The oak tree outside the window has many branches that are forked. If I were a squirrel, I could go so far along such a branch, but when I arrived at the fork, I would have to choose which direction to follow. Sometimes my choice is guided by the presence of something I desire which is to be found along one of the 'branches' and not, apparently, along the other. As a squirrel, for example, I might choose the branch that seems to lead to more acorns. Sometimes the choice seems entirely random, guided only by my intuition, or the whim of the moment.

Often these everyday choices are unimportant. But sometimes major issues are involved, concerning life and relationship decisions. And the more that is at stake, the more tempting it is to assume that one 'branch' is 'right' and all other options are 'wrong'. That makes it much easier for me to choose, and to stay with my choice in the future. I can't be on two branches at once, so the more firmly I can justify my choice, the better.

Unfortunately, these assumptions about the 'right' and the 'wrong' way are usually ill-founded. Life is rarely black and white. The best we can often do is to choose the branch that is more life-giving for us right now, but to hold that choice in the light of a deeper understanding that other branches may be the more life-giving choice for other people or in different situations. And that is where the forked branches in the oak tree become my wise teachers. They show me how all the branches can be traced back to a 'deeper root'. There is a point, further down the tree, where they are one. Their separateness is merely a manifestation of a deeper oneness in the base of the branch, in the trunk, and in the tap root.

The tap root is what keeps the tree alive. And the same is true for our 'soul survival'. At the 'branch' level of our existence, anything can happen. There are no guarantees, no insurance policies. Storms might rip through our branches, or lightning might set them on fire. The heat of the sun might split them or blight might kill them. Yet the 'tree' of our being is rooted in God, and that tap root lies too deep to be subject to the volatile world above ground. Even more than this, our tap root is something that is common to us all. The deeper we go in our journeying with God, the closer we come together, at home in the ground of our being, far deeper than the 'fences' that divide us. At that depth we share intimately in each other's struggles, and we are nourished by each other's trust.

At these depths, there is often darkness. We do not, and cannot, know how our growing is working itself out, or how long it will take before we come into the fullness of our being. But the tap root is the source of all the nourishment we need to keep us going through the dark unknowing. We can connect to this tap root in the silence of prayer, asking God simply to hold us in the darkness, to feed us in ways we cannot understand or explain.

'Like a tree planted by water, sending out its roots by the stream'

During the Second World War, many Londoners survived the blitz by 'going deep', into the underground, where bombs could not penetrate. Life can still feel like a bombing raid, even in peace time. Job security can disappear overnight, and the pension funds that our old-age provision depends on can be wiped out at the click of a mouse on a finance company's computer screen. Disease can strike us down. Friends can betray us and lovers abandon us. Perhaps you know some of these 'bombs' in your own life. Where do you seek shelter in these circumstances? When the sirens of misfortune wail through your life, do you know the way to the underground?

In war time, everyone knew their way to the nearest air-raid shelter. Their survival depended on it. In the same way, the survival of your deepest being depends on your knowing how to draw life-strength from your deepest roots. Where are those roots for you? What sustains you when everything else lets you down? If the branches of your life—those projects or relationships that you value—are struck by lightning, where is your tap root? What connects you to the ground of your being? How familiar are you with the access routes to that deeper root? One way to become familiar with the way down to your tap root is to keep using it, in prayer, until eventually it will be second nature to you and you will be able to find it in the darkest night.

Lord, I live 'above ground' for most of my waking moments. Teach me the way to my tap root in you. Clear the deepest channels of my being so that your love and grace can flow freely to the exposed edges of my living. Amen

Surrender

Yet, O Lord, you are our Father;
we are the clay, and you are our potter;
we are all the work of your hand.
ISAIAH 64:8

The word that came to Jeremiah from the Lord: 'Come, go down to
the potter's house, and there I will let you hear my words.' So I went
down to the potter's house, and there he was working at his wheel.
The vessel he was making of clay was spoiled in the potter's hand,
and he reworked it into another vessel, as seemed good to him.

Then the word of the Lord came to me: 'Can I not do with you,
O house of Israel, just as this potter has done?' says the Lord. 'Just like
clay in the potter's hand, so are you in my hand, O house of Israel.'
JEREMIAH 18:1–6

A friend of mine, who is blind, recently made a visit to a
local pottery manufacturer, where visitors were invited
to try their hand at the potter's wheel and experience for
themselves how it would feel to mould and shape a lump of
clay. To make this possible for my friend, the potter who was
demonstrating his craft offered to work with him. And so my
friend described to me afterwards the experience of feeling
the wet clay beneath his hands, but also the gentle strength
of the potter's hands guiding his own, as they shaped the clay
together.

This story helps me to relate in a new way to the image of
God as the Potter. It also leads me to reflect on whose hands
are forming my life. Are they God's hands, and the hands

of those who help to shape me in and through God's love? Or are they the hands of other people, waiting in the wings to shape me into a mould that suits their own purposes? Or are there perhaps no guiding hands at all, because I am sometimes so determined to do it all my way?

I came to the conclusion that for much of my life I have allowed—and continue to allow—other factors to shape me in ways that may not be God's ways. Sometimes these are other people who may or may not mean well, and could be misguided, or even manipulative, in their clumsy attempts to mould the clay of my life. Sometimes these alien factors may be circumstances that I meet, which I too often allow to shape my course in ways that, on deeper reflection, I might not have chosen.

Small wonder, then, that my 'pot' so often turns pear-shaped! And God, as Jeremiah reminds us, has to begin again, flattening out the mess and reshaping it over and over, with endless patience. Would that I had that kind of patience too! The waiting time seems to last for ever, punctuated by one failed pot after another and a long process of reshaping and re-forming.

How can I learn to trust this process more deeply? When my life is, so to speak, on the potter's wheel, trust is often a long way from my heart. The wheel of circumstances spins so wildly, it seems. The pressure of the potter's hands, so firm and gentle when God is the Potter, can sometimes take me almost to breaking point when those hands are not God's. I feel only the pressure and the dizziness. How can I trust that the Potter knows what he is doing?

One thing that helps me to discern when my life is being shaped by the eternal Potter is the purpose of the pot as it starts to take shape. A pot is made to hold something, and to offer that something to others—food or drink, perhaps, or flowers. When God's hand is guiding the circumstances of my life, the result will be something for others, however small. God the Potter is God the Giver. To trust the process that leads to this result, I am asked to surrender my own limited thoughts and views of what should happen to the larger vision of the holy Potter, who knows what he is making and why.

Would that we could always let God do the shaping, trusting in God's vision when we ourselves have as yet no clue to what is becoming of us. We fail, of course. Over and over we surrender our freedom to the wrong hands, or we claim the right to shape ourselves, and God begins again. But today's readings give us hope that getting things wrong is never the final word. Reshaping is always a possibility. God doesn't power down the wheel at clocking-off time and go home in despair. The very fact that my failures and breakdowns happen is another sign that God is the master Potter, however many other would-be potters, including myself, interfere with the process.

Yesterday we found a source of trustfulness by going to a deeper root of our being. Today we discover trust in the simple fact that the potter knows better than the clay. Ultimately, the clay has no choice but to surrender to the potter's hands. Certainly, we can resist the potter's touch, just as a child can resist the guidance of a loving parent. But our resistance can, at worst, only prolong the process of our becoming. It has no power to override the potter's vision for his new creation.

'Like the clay in the potter's hand, so are you in my hand'

Try shaping a piece of clay in your hands or, if this isn't possible, try to imagine yourself doing so. That shaping is helped greatly by the warmth of your hands, and by their moisture. Where does the warmth come from in the shaping of your life? Where is the moisture? Perhaps your tears are a necessary ingredient.

The process through which God is shaping God's dream in our lives is always done by hand. It is a process of intimate contact. Intimacy requires trust, as it invites us to surrender to the touch of God's love, so deeply personal, shaping us uniquely. No mass production on God's workbench; no two pots alike in God's kingdom; and, in the end, no waste!

Lord, I ask for the grace to love you enough to trust you, and to trust you enough to let you shape me into someone who will offer your love back to your creation. Amen

Simplicity

[Jesus] said to his disciples, 'Therefore I tell you, do not worry about your life, what you will eat, or about your body, what you will wear. For life is more than food, and the body more than clothing. Consider the ravens: they neither sow nor reap, they have neither storehouse nor barn, and yet God feeds them. Of how much more value are you than the birds! And can any of you by worrying add a single hour to your span of life? If then you are not able to do so small a thing as that, why do you worry about the rest? Consider the lilies, how they grow: they neither toil nor spin, yet I tell you, even Solomon in all his glory was not clothed like one of these. But if God so clothes the grass of the field, which is alive today and tomorrow is thrown into the oven, how much more will he clothe you—you of little faith! And do not keep striving for what you are to eat and what you are to drink, and do not keep worrying. For it is the nations of the world that strive after all these things, and your Father knows that you need them. Instead, strive for his kingdom, and these things will be given to you as well. Do not be afraid, little flock, for it is your Father's pleasure to give you the kingdom.'
LUKE 12:22–32

Two surprises dropped into my life recently, one good and one not so good.

First, the bad news. This came in the form of a statement from a trust fund we have, that is supposed to be paying for our daughter's years in medical school. The statement informed me that the fund isn't doing very well at all.

With a wry smile I remembered the small print—that investments like these can go down as well as up. I thought about all those people in the City, sitting at their PCs, clicking their way through rows and rows of figures. I thought about all the fund managers in their smart suits, weighing up the relative prospects of this company or the other, and moving money around the world in some endless poker game, stressing themselves into heart attacks and strokes. I thought of all the board meetings and shareholders' gatherings, debating what to do through every new crisis.

The end result of all my pondering came to zero. There is absolutely nothing I can do to make the fund more fruitful. Nor does it appear to be possible for all those busy executives to 'add a single hour' to its existence! So I may as well get on with my life and stop worrying.

But the good news went a long way to make up for this setback. At the end of the garden is a field. The farmer who works it has had a bad year. The weather has been unkind to him. The crop he sowed in spring failed and had to be ploughed in again. Now the field is green with a grass crop, just as the autumn is settling in.

The surprise came in the shape of a magnificent sunflower, standing proud, right in the middle of this field—all alone, in solitary splendour! For some time we have watched this little 'alien' growing there, a spot of darker green among the grass. Eventually it became obvious that it was going to be something special, and this week it came into its glory. Its dinner-plate flower is fully open now, exuberantly golden, its head raised proudly to the skies, lord of all it surveys.

Back in the wet, dark days of last autumn, a sunflower seed must have dropped into the soggy furrows of that field. No one knew about the event. The farmer had no idea it was there, and nor did we—though I suspect God may have had an inkling of what was happening!

Through the wind and rain of winter it germinated down there in the field. No one helped it along. No one brought any fertiliser or put it in a greenhouse. It just got on with the job of becoming what it was always meant to be—unheard, unseen, unregarded—until when the time was right it thrust its whole being through the clay soil and presented itself to creation.

While the sunflower was in bloom, we had a group of people in our home for a quiet day. At the end of the day they were sharing their reflections on what the day's quiet prayer had meant for them, and every one of them had something to say about that sunflower. 'A messenger from God,' one person described it. 'Just to remind us that God is making us into the people God dreams us to be, without any of our own doing.'

'A sign for me,' said another, 'that the seed that no one planted and no one tended can become the most beautiful growth in the whole field.'

'A promise,' suggested a third, 'that if God can delight and surprise us with a solitary sunflower in a field, how much more can this happen in *our* lives, if we will only allow it.'

'I tell you, do not worry about your life'

Look back over how your week has been so far. What has bogged you down and sent you into 'worry mode'? Have there been any 'sunflowers' around, to remind you that trusting God to grow you into who you really are is almost too simple to be true?

Lord of the stock markets and the sunflower seeds, give me the grace to trust the silent growth of your seed in my heart and to let that trust grow stronger and taller than all my worries. Amen

Obedience

On the third day there was a wedding in Cana of Galilee, and the mother of Jesus was there. Jesus and his disciples had also been invited to the wedding. When the wine gave out, the mother of Jesus said to him, 'They have no wine.' And Jesus said to her, 'Woman, what concern is that to you and to me? My hour has not yet come.' His mother said to the servants, 'Do whatever he tells you.'

Now standing there were six stone water-jars for the Jewish rites of purification, each holding twenty or thirty gallons. Jesus said to them, 'Fill the jars with water.' And they filled them up to the brim. He said to them, 'Now draw some out, and take it to the chief steward.' So they took it. When the steward tasted the water that had become wine, and did not know where it had come from (though the servants who had drawn the water knew), the steward called the bridegroom and said to him, 'Everyone serves the good wine first, and then the inferior wine after the guests have become drunk. But you have kept the good wine until now.' Jesus did this, the first of his signs, in Cana of Galilee, and revealed his glory; and his disciples believed in him.

JOHN 2:1–11

In my youth, like many children, I guess, I frequently demanded to know why I was being asked to do something or, more often, to refrain from doing something—to which the parental reply would come back, 'Because I say so!' At the time I promised myself that I would never give such unsatisfactory answers to my own children but, needless to say, I failed in that undertaking!

Here we find Jesus himself, or rather his mother on his behalf, saying very much the same kind of thing. 'Don't ask questions. Just do it! Do as he tells you!' It sounds like a demand for blind obedience, which raises big questions in the minds of generations who have witnessed the horrors of the Holocaust, and the extremes of abuse into which blind obedience can lead. And yet here, at Cana, this demand for obedience was the necessary condition for Jesus' first miracle, the first manifestation of his power to transform.

When is it appropriate to obey, and when is it right to resist? When should we remain within legitimate boundaries and when is it our duty to break out of oppressive limitations? I find it fascinating to discover Jesus himself grappling with these thoughts, when his mother first points out to him that the wine has run out. At first he seems to want to stay within the boundaries. 'Why are you telling me this? Don't challenge me to take action here. It's not the right time.' But Mary's intuition prevails, that this is indeed the right time and that God's transforming power is beginning to flow, through her son. She acts on her intuition and issues the instruction to 'do whatever he tells you'. With this, it seems, Jesus is pushed over the boundary and the latent power of God within him is released. He becomes obedient to the demands of this new power, and the servants, in their turn, proceed to do as they have been told with unquestioning obedience. The obedience both of Jesus to his Father and of the servants to Jesus is based on *trust*. But at this point, that trust is a blind one. None of them can predict or imagine where this act of obedience is going to lead.

The question of power and authority is high on the world's agenda today, and it is the source of much heart-searching within the Church too. 'Power' is a loaded word. Perhaps it is so loaded because, for the most part, we experience the exercise of power in our world as an oppressive force, enslaving people, engendering fear, and centred on the 'kingdom' of the power wielder, rather than on the reign of God. We see it, justifiably, as the *power to control*. We know that such power cannot be trusted and we instinctively want to resist.

At Cana, however, a very different kind of power is being released—the *power to transform*. Jesus' ability to change the water into wine is a sign—the first sign—of God's unimaginable power to transform our broken creation into an eternity of love and of life. Jesus is very far from wanting to 'control' the situation, as his hesitation reveals. But he is willing to obey the promptings of the Father to open up a channel of transformation. When transformation is the source and the intention of power, obedience is the appropriate response—even blind obedience, because we are being touched here by things we cannot begin to understand, yet know we can trust and are called to cooperate with.

Through the miracle at Cana, Jesus 'revealed his glory' and the disciples, we learn, 'believed in him'. The power that transforms inspires our trust. This kind of power flows from authentic 'authority'. The authority of Jesus is rooted in the Father, the Author of all being. This is the only kind of authority we are asked to trust, but we are asked to trust it completely, and be obedient to its action in our lives and in our hearts.

'Do whatever he tells you'

Who, or what, exerts power in your life? In what ways is obedience expected of you, and what is the agenda behind this expectation?

Without making any judgements, either of yourself or of others, just notice:

- What channels of power and authority in your life are tending to control and enslave you in some way, engendering fear and serving the agenda of someone else's 'kingdom'? How do you feel about your reaction to these power centres?
- Where do you see evidence of transforming power in your life? (Perhaps in significant relationships, or the demands of a life-giving cause or project.) In what ways do you feel you are being asked to cooperate with this kind of power, maybe without any explanations in advance as to how it will all work out?

Lord, open our eyes to recognise and resist the powers that seek to control us, but to trust and cooperate with your power that longs to transform us. Amen

Adventure

The next day John again was standing with two of his disciples, and as he watched Jesus walk by, he exclaimed, 'Look, here is the Lamb of God!' The two disciples heard him say this, and they followed Jesus. When Jesus turned and saw them following, he said to them, 'What are you looking for?' They said to him, 'Rabbi' (which translated means Teacher), 'where are you staying?' He said to them, 'Come and see.' They came and saw where he was staying, and they remained with him that day.
JOHN 1:35–39

Every tiny step in the process of evolution is a step beyond the comfort zone—and every such step is a step taken in trust. Since the first primitive sea creatures set tentative foot on the hazardous terrain of dry land, all creation has been moving and growing in this global adventure of life. Our spiritual growth, surely, is no exception to this universal pattern.

I grew up before aliens, dinosaurs and disaster movies took over the TV screens, in the days when major epics centred on the journeys of pioneers across America in wagon trains. I remember watching, fascinated, as families would sell everything they owned in order to buy the wagon and the oxen and a few pots and pans for the trek west, across completely uncharted land. Then, with only the wisdom and courage of a scout to help them find the way and protect themselves against whatever dangers they might encounter, they would set out on journeys of thousands of miles, to follow their dream.

'What vision might be worth a venture like that?' I ask myself. For those early pioneers, the vision that impelled them onwards was perhaps about freedom, a new start in a new world, and riches and well-being that were unimaginable in the slums of Europe or downtown New York. It was also an expression of the insatiable quest in humankind to know what lies beyond our present experience. Perhaps this quest is right at the heart of everything we call 'adventure'.

An adventure is about to happen on the morning described in today's reading. Its beginnings are very modest. The curious gaze of two young men follows the steps of a travelling rabbi. The man who has been their leader until now makes no attempt to hold them back. Instead, he urges them to follow the stranger. They have no rational way of knowing that this man Jesus will lead them to their deepest desiring. We, who follow after, know that the quest into which Jesus leads us is also about freedom, a new start in a world God is renewing, and a spiritual wealth and well-being beyond anything we could ever provide for ourselves. He invites us, just as he invited them, into the great adventure of 'come and see'. For us the terrain of this journey is by no means as unknown as it was for John's disciples, yet it remains God's mystery. For each of us the adventure will take a different route. But it will always call us beyond our comfort zone.

We might notice three 'steps to adventure' in this story:

- We need the courage to take just that first step in pursuit of our dream.
- We need to reflect on what is really at the heart of our dream. What do we want?
- We need to follow, with complete trust, wherever the dream may lead.

The disciples take the first step to discover who this man is, who so holds their attention. When they follow him, he challenges them with the question 'What do you want?' and invites them to make a journey of trust, without telling them where it will lead. 'Come and see,' he says.

One important way in which we exercise trust is by stepping out in courage. To take that first step in following our dream is an act of trust. Trust is not necessarily a state of passivity, but often one of expectant readiness. To trust in the one who calls us to 'come and see' is to be ready, if necessary, to let go of everything we thought was so important, in order to have the resources to 'buy our wagon' and move on.

A wise adventurer travels light. The early American pioneers who had loaded up their wagons with all kinds of extras were the ones who got stuck on the steep gradients and had to jettison the things they hadn't been able to leave behind them. When they follow Jesus, John's disciples are leaving behind the people, places and situations that have until then provided them with identity and security. Our own journey of trust may ask no less of us. The more 'baggage' we are carrying with us, in terms of emotional or material 'dependencies', the more likely we are to come unstuck at the first major hurdle. Can we trust the One who calls us enough to let everything else in our lives slip into second place behind our deepest desire to be discoverers and co-creators of God's reign on earth?

'Come and see'

What form has the 'adventure of faith' taken for you, so far, in your life? Look back, if you can, to the very first steps, and remember the trust in which you set out. What vision inspired you? Can you see any ways in which your trust has strengthened with each subsequent step along the way?

The particular path you are walking has never been walked before. You are pioneering it, with Jesus as your 'scout'. You are learning to trust him. Stop to reflect today on just how much he trusts you to pioneer your personal route through the tangle of creation, so that God's grace may flow freely through that unique combination of circumstances.

Lord, I don't know where we are going, but I trust your invitation to 'come and see'. Give me the courage to invest everything I have and everything I am in the great adventure of life in you. Amen

Dreaming

Now the birth of Jesus the Messiah took place in this way. When his mother Mary had been engaged to Joseph, but before they lived together, she was found to be with child from the Holy Spirit. Her husband Joseph, being a righteous man and unwilling to expose her to public disgrace, planned to dismiss her quietly. But just when he had resolved to do this, an angel of the Lord appeared to him in a dream and said, 'Joseph, son of David, do not be afraid to take Mary as your wife, for the child conceived in her is from the Holy Spirit. She will bear a son, and you are to name him Jesus, for he will save his people from their sins.' All this took place to fulfil what had been spoken by the Lord through the prophet: 'Look, the virgin shall conceive and bear a son, and they shall name him Emmanuel', which means, 'God is with us.' When Joseph awoke from sleep, he did as the angel of the Lord commanded him; he took her as his wife, but had no marital relations with her until she had borne a son; and he named him Jesus.

MATTHEW 1:18–25

How close the connections, it sometimes seems, between our dreams and our nightmares! Today we are reminded of the nightmare that was unfolding in Joseph's life as a result of Mary's pregnancy. It may help you to empathise with his situation if you can recall any major crisis in your own life, and the many conflicting feelings it brought up in you, along with all the agonised heart-searching about what to do and how to respond to the changed circumstances.

It is perhaps all too easy to leave Mary and Joseph safely

and cosily in the tableau of the school nativity play. Looking into the real heartache and very present dangers that faced them as a direct result of Mary's 'Yes' to God is often something we would rather avoid.

Yet the way through this apparent deadlock—this nightmare that must end, at the very least, in a heart-breaking divorce—opens up, paradoxically, in a dream. The story records how Joseph came to a deeper understanding of God's meaning in this confusion when he was fast asleep. When his normal conscious thought processes were in abeyance, Joseph's heart became receptive to new possibilities— possibilities that defied reason, yet rang deeply true. This story holds out more hope for us, today, than perhaps we even dare to imagine.

We don't need to search too far to discover our own 21st-century incarnations of Joseph's nightmare. At a personal level we grapple with our own difficult relationships, conflicts and moral dilemmas. As a human family together, we face sudden and terrible upheavals from both natural and man-made disasters. Our certainties, hopes and expectations can be dashed overnight, like sandcastles on the seashore. What can we do when life takes us by the throat in this kind of way, and squeezes the very breath out of us? Well, in his own way, Joseph knew the flavour of that personal nightmare. And for him the deeper answer lay concealed within a dream.

To get in touch with the deeper dream, it may be necessary to change gear and focus not on the feelings that were aroused by the tragedy itself, but rather on any new life that ultimately grew from it. There are trees in the Australian outback that are regularly destroyed by forest fires. Yet the forests regenerate over and over again. They do so because their seeds burst open only when they are exposed to the kind of high temperatures that occur in a fire. The coming of new growth is built into the tree's nature. The dream of the new life is latent in the ashes of the old.

If we take a look at some of our own tragedies in this light—either personal or global—we may detect similar new growth. Personal break-down often releases a new spurt of personal growth, the development of a new depth of wisdom and compassion, or new insights into alternative ways forward. Global disaster can release the very best in humankind—the overwhelming and universal desire to preserve the sanctity of life, to rescue those in danger, to comfort and tend those who are hurt or in grief. The dream of all that is best in us is latent in the wreckage of the worst we can do to each other.

So today's reading might lead us to reflect that one way to deal with the nightmare scenarios in our life can be to go deeper, down to the layers of our being that lie below politics and cultural patterning, there to discover the fragments of God that inhabit our hearts and draw us together, in our common humanity, when circumstances seem to be hurling us apart.

We must thank God that Joseph does not act out of the nightmare going on at the surface of his life, but out of the dream that inhabits the core of his being. If he had stayed with the surface nightmare, he might well have wanted to lash out in anger against the unseen, unknown father of his fiancée's child. A ludicrous idea? Yet one we all too easily embody in our own 'surface' thinking and reacting—and history teaches us the results. The dream reveals another way.

And Joseph, in his zero hour, when his hopes of marriage, his faith, and his relationship with the girl he loves have crumbled into dust, teaches us how to make that other way a reality in our own lives. He trusts the dream; and he acts upon it.

'An angel of the Lord appeared to him in a dream'

Take time this week to look at a newspaper. You will read about some aspect of 'the nightmare' for sure, but notice too the scattered evidence of the deeper dream—the God-with-us, the 'best' that is at the core of our being and is always there, like a silent angel, for those who have eyes to see. Which will you trust? Which will you act upon?

Lord, below the world's nightmares lies your indestructible dream. We catch glimpses of it in moments of compassion, heroism, resilience and all expressions of authentic human loving. Give us the grace to trust the dream, especially when it seems to be buried in the ash and debris of our lives. Amen

15–21 December

Glimpses of Wisdom

Not all guidance comes from outside ourselves. There is also a pool of deep wisdom in the core of our being, and we can learn to discern what within ourselves can be trusted and what cannot. During the next few days we focus on the slow growth of that wisdom and that discernment, and how we might cooperate in its growth.

We begin by joining Mary as she makes her response to God's action in her life in the words of the Magnificat—an expression that surrenders itself to the greater reality within and beyond itself, and lets that wisdom spill out to touch all creation.

- Our search for the wisdom that is God's own wisdom then leads us to discover how much wider and deeper is God's perspective, relative to our own (15 December)
- We join Solomon in his discerning of what makes for true wisdom (16 December)
- We look at which 'seeds' in our life are growing into wholesome harvest, and which are not (17 December)
- We allow God to 'grow' us, by moving us gently beyond our comfort zones (18 December)
- We explore what it means to wait 'in readiness' for God's Advent into our lives (19 December)

- We reflect on how personal suffering can draw us into deeper levels of wisdom and understanding (20 December)
- And, finally, we share in the meeting between Mary and Elizabeth, and learn from them the power of recognising in each other the Christ who is coming to birth in each of us (21 December)

Perspective

My soul magnifies the Lord,
and my spirit rejoices in God my Saviour,
for he has looked with favour on the lowliness of his servant.
Surely, from now on all generations will call me blessed;
for the Mighty One has done great things for me,
and holy is his name.
His mercy is for those who fear him
from generation to generation.
He has shown strength with his arm;
he has scattered the proud in the thoughts of their hearts.
He has brought down the powerful from their thrones,
and lifted up the lowly;
he has filled the hungry with good things,
and sent the rich away empty.
He has helped his servant Israel,
in remembrance of his mercy,
according to the promise he made to our ancestors,
to Abraham and to his descendants for ever.
LUKE 1:46–55

With these words of prayer and praise, Mary begins her personal 'waiting time', and we might allow them to lead us into what it means for us personally to be waiting, expectantly as she is, for the coming of God into our lives and our world.

The child she is carrying has already upturned her world, her hopes of a quiet life, even her religious expectations. It's one thing to believe in the coming of the Messiah who will become the liberator of his people Israel—it's quite another matter to be invited to bring that Messiah to birth oneself! All that is going to happen in the thirty or so years that lie ahead will challenge Mary's expectations over and over again. Events will move her, at breakneck speed, beyond the 'received wisdom' that has come to her from the teachings of the Jewish faith and her family upbringing, to a radically new kind of wisdom that will emerge from the depths of her own heart, under the guidance of the Spirit of the child she carries.

This process of gaining a very different perspective on God's wisdom begins the moment Jesus is conceived in her. From this moment, Mary's understanding of God's ways widens and deepens. It is a perspective that goes right back to her spiritual roots, and the roots of her people, but also extends far forwards to a kingdom that is yet to come.

In a few days' time we will spend some time with Hannah, who prayed for a child, whose prayer was granted, and who then gave that child, Samuel, over to the Lord's service. Hannah, too, when she knew that she was at last pregnant with Samuel, expressed her joy in a prayer very similar to Mary's Magnificat (see 1 Samuel 2:1–10). Luke makes sure we make this connection in our minds, by stressing the similarities between both women's prayers. Mary is speaking the language of her forebears in faith in her thanksgiving to God. Implicitly, she too is acknowledging that her child is also given over to the Lord, whatever that may come to mean for her as the years unfold.

So there is a looking back, and a looking forward. When a child is born, this extended perspective is always evident. People look for family traits and resemblances in the new life, and they also express hopes for its future. Often threads of family connectedness are rewoven at such a time, but, for the parents at least, there is a radical change to their future expectations. Anyone whose life has ever been touched by the presence of a new baby knows what power such a tiny being has to overturn and unsettle us. Wisdom begins to dawn that human life is both utterly fragile and vulnerable, and utterly awesome in its power to shape and transform creation. We stand before the mystery that everything we are, as individuals, began long before human memory, when God's love first spilled over into creation, and extends far beyond our own lifespan, affecting, for good or ill, everything and everyone following after us. We also realise that this private event for a particular family is always a public event as well, with the potential to shape the course of human evolution in some unique way. Every birth is both a moment in history and a manifestation of mystery. This is wisdom that God grants to every human heart that has ever beheld the wonder of new life.

The novelist Victor Hugo once commented that 'more powerful than all the armies in the world is an idea whose time is come'. You may recognise in your own life those projects that were unstoppable because 'the time was right', while ideas that you may have desperately strained to bring to fruition came to nothing if their time had not yet come. As we pause alongside Mary at the moment of Jesus' conception, we are witnessing the moment when God's idea has come to its time. Life itself is God's idea, and this Christ-child is given to us to bring life in all its fullness. That fullness will be a kingdom where gentleness prevails over force, humility over arrogance, simplicity over extravagance. The time has come. Nothing on earth can stop the fulfilling of God's idea, now that Mary has said her 'Yes'. The divine revolution is under way!

'The Mighty One has done great things for me'

What begins with Mary's 'Yes' is to be continued in every human life, until Alpha evolves into Omega and all creation is restored to its original wholeness. Each of us is invited, in a unique way, to engage our life's energy in the great venture of making God's idea a reality in our world. Take a moment to reflect on the times in your life when you have become aware of the radical wisdom of God touching your life in some particular way—perhaps a moment of insight, or the certainty that a particular choice should be made. What difference have such times made to you? Write your personal 'Magnificat', if you feel drawn to do so.

Lord, take all that we have received from the past, and grow and transform it into all that we shall become, in the fullness of the kingdom. Amen

Discernment

The king went to Gibeon to sacrifice there, for that was the principal high place; Solomon used to offer a thousand burnt offerings on that altar. At Gibeon the Lord appeared to Solomon in a dream by night; and God said, 'Ask what I should give you.' And Solomon said, 'You have shown great and steadfast love to your servant my father David, because he walked before you in faithfulness, in righteousness, and in uprightness of heart toward you; and you have kept for him this great and steadfast love, and have given him a son to sit on his throne today. And now, O Lord my God, you have made your servant king in place of my father David, although I am only a little child; I do not know how to go out or come in. And your servant is in the midst of the people whom you have chosen, a great people, so numerous they cannot be numbered or counted. Give your servant therefore an understanding mind to govern your people, able to discern between good and evil; for who can govern this your great people?'

It pleased the Lord that Solomon had asked this. God said to him, 'Because you have asked this, and have not asked for yourself long life or riches, or for the life of your enemies, but have asked for yourself understanding to discern what is right, I now do according to your word. Indeed I give you a wise and discerning mind; no one like you has been before you and no one like you shall arise after you. I give you also what you have not asked, both riches and honour all your life; no other king shall compare with you. If you will walk in my ways, keeping my statutes and my commandments, as your father David walked, then I will lengthen your life.'

Then Solomon awoke; it had been a dream. He came to Jerusalem, where he stood before the ark of the covenant of the Lord. He offered up burnt offerings and offerings of well-being, and provided a feast for all his servants.

1 KINGS 3:4–15

Yesterday, Mary's Magnificat gave us a starting point for our exploration of what it means to be waiting for God's wisdom, by showing us that whatever this wisdom is about, it is rooted in our own humility. To the extent that we can begin to recognise the impossibility of bringing anything to birth on our own, so we become open to God's action in our living. To the extent that we remain determined to 'do our own thing' in our own way, we block that action.

Today Solomon is dreaming! Deep in his psyche lies the overwhelming question of how he can possibly cope with the demands that are coming down on him. He has become king in succession to his illustrious father David, but, as he confesses, he has really no idea what to do next. He is young, inexperienced in leadership, and feels very much the shadow of his father hanging over every move he makes. I wonder how we would react to a newly elected prime minister who had the honesty to confess his or her feelings of inadequacy with such disarming candour. I hope we would welcome it as a sign that at last our national and international relations might have a chance of beginning from a place of integrity and humility.

Dare we risk being so vulnerable before God, let alone in the hearing of those we want to admire us? Solomon's dream urges him to take this risk. In the dream, God invites him to choose the gift he most wants, to help him master the challenges that lie ahead.

Well, life for a king would be easier, certainly, if his enemies were all eliminated. The power to scare away all opposition is a very tempting gift. We choose it every time we invest our resources in weapons of defence, at the expense of the tools of growth and well-being. We choose it every time we silence or diminish an ethnic minority in our society or condone violence against them, or 'put down' a friend or colleague.

Then again, for the power wielder who doesn't want blood on his hands, a welcome gift would be the financial resources to 'buy off' anyone who poses a threat. With these resources, commercial exploitation can replace weapons of war, leaving less visible, but no less real, carnage in its wake. At a personal level, a gift like this enables us to purchase 'friendship', to appease potential hostility and to ensure that we live among like-minded people.

And then, of course, to enjoy the security and comfort we have purchased with our gifts of power and wealth, we need the extra bonus of a long life in which to enjoy it.

Solomon says, 'No.' The temptations are obvious, but Solomon's dream points to another way. He chooses the gift of a discerning heart, to judge rightly the better way of dealing with every situation that life may throw at him as a leader, and as an individual human being. Such a gift offers absolutely no insurance against the 'enemy at the door' and no guarantee of a comfortable lifestyle. What it holds out to us is the possibility of living our own lives, both publicly and privately, in a way that is centred not on our fears or our greed, but on the deep wisdom of God.

The gift is gladly granted. And what God bestows on Solomon is bestowed with equal joy on everyone who honestly wants 'wisdom' to be the first priority in their living, and the prime yardstick for their choices and decisions. The dream goes further: if we were truly able to make every choice based on this deeper discernment, aligned to the wisdom of God, we would discover that our lesser priorities would also fall into place, and our human need for security and comfort would be satisfied without the need to exploit or threaten each other.

'Ask what I should give you'

Let God put the same question to you that was put to Solomon. What one gift would you ask for, as the greatest help in dealing with the choices and events and relationships in your life right now? Don't answer too hastily. Consider carefully all the options, and acknowledge whatever fears and needs they reveal, bringing them to God in the centre of honesty and vulnerability at the core of your being.

Lord, when we don't know what we want, please give us
the one thing that we really need. Amen

Seeds

[Jesus] also said, 'The kingdom of God is as if someone would scatter seed on the ground, and would sleep and rise night and day, and the seed would sprout and grow, he does not know how. The earth produces of itself, first the stalk, then the head, then the full grain in the head. But when the grain is ripe, at once he goes in with his sickle, because the harvest has come.'

He also said, 'With what can we compare the kingdom of God, or what parable will we use for it? It is like a mustard seed, which, when sown upon the ground, is the smallest of all the seeds on earth; yet when it is sown it grows up and becomes the greatest of all shrubs, and puts forth large branches, so that the birds of the air can make nests in its shade.'

MARK 4:26–32

Wisdom grows slowly! Often we might well feel that God's wisdom in our hearts is not growing at all. Much as we may desire to follow Solomon in asking God for the gift, above all, of a discerning heart and wise judgement in all we do, more often than not we act on different priorities entirely. Even more disturbingly, we frequently find that the roots of the bad things that happen to us lead back to choices we, or others, made in the past, that were based not on wisdom but on fear or the desire for personal gain. What grows from these flawed seeds may overwhelm us with the ferocity of what it yields when harvest time comes round.

When we listen to the international news, we can discover, almost every night, the evidence of some deadly crop that is growing in the world's fields because in earlier times we have sown bad seed like this. The crimes and even the mistakes and misjudgements of past generations fester on, and continue to haunt our efforts to make our world a place of peace and mutual respect. The abused child can become a child abuser. The violated victim can turn into a violent oppressor of others.

In the musical *Les Misérables*, the boy revolutionary Gavroche puts these warnings into a song which reminds us that if we abuse a dog while it is just a puppy, we should beware of what may happen when the pup becomes a full-grown Rottweiler!

We all know that if we sow the wind we will reap the whirlwind. Tragically, one generation's 'wind' becomes the next generation's 'whirlwind'. And the growth from breeze to hurricane happens so stealthily that we never see it coming.

If such terrible consequences can grow from the 'bad seeds' we sow when we are not living in the light of a higher wisdom, what good fruits, in contrast, might grow from the seeds of love and justice and hope that we sow?

Last night I had a phone call from my oldest friend to tell me that her mother, Alice, had died. We shared our sorrow across an international phone line, and as we were reminiscing, I remembered, so vividly, an incident from our childhood. I was a frequent visitor then at my friend's home, and her parents always made me feel very welcome. One afternoon, we were all sitting in their house looking out over their back garden, and Alice drew my attention to a riot of exotic growth in the flowerbed in the middle of their little back lawn. It looked like something out of the botanical gardens. There were flowers there that none of us had ever seen before. 'Where on earth did they all come from?' I asked, mystified. Alice pointed to the bird table at the edge of the flowerbed. 'Last winter I got some bird seed and put it out there for the birds to help themselves. I guess they must have dropped some, and this is what it grew into!'

We laughed, then, at the amazing harvest that had grown, so slowly and steadily through the winter months, to yield such a crop. And last night, too, on the phone, our tears began to turn into a glimmer of returning joy as we remembered other seeds that Alice had sown, perhaps unknowingly, in our childhood experience. Seeds of compassion and integrity, the love that cherishes and the faith that keeps going. I can easily see the harvest of those seeds now in my friend's life, which is dedicated to God and God's people in ways she is too humble to see for herself.

Today we reap the harvest of Alice's seeding, all those years ago, and we in our turn are asked to plough these good seeds back into the earth we will one day leave behind, so that generations still unborn will also rejoice in unexpected blossoms. The process is continuous. The product is beyond our sight. But the choice, to sow good or bad seed in any given situation, is ours to make, day by day.

'The seed would sprout and grow,
he does not know how'

For most of us, the 'flowerbed' of our lives will contain a bewildering mixture of weeds and blossoms. Take a while to wander round your own life's 'flowerbed', just noticing what is growing there. If you see things you don't like and would like to uproot, notice what seeds they have grown from, and ask God to do any weeding that is needful. Rejoice in the blossoms and fruits. What seeds have given life to these good things? Express your thanks in whatever way feels right.

You can be sure of one thing: good fruit can only come from good seed. Whatever is fruitful and life-giving in your experience is coming, ultimately, from God, the source of life. Whatever is destructive is coming from things that are not rooted in God. Let what you find shape tomorrow's choices in some specific way.

Lord, please give us the grace to look carefully, in the light of your wisdom, at the seeds we scatter in the course of our daily living, that they may become a good and wholesome harvest for those who will reap what we sow. Amen

Growth

In due time Hannah conceived and bore a son. She named him Samuel, for she said, 'I have asked him of the Lord.'

The man Elkanah and all his household went up to offer to the Lord the yearly sacrifice, and to pay his vow. But Hannah did not go up, for she said to her husband, 'As soon as the child is weaned, I will bring him, that he may appear in the presence of the Lord, and remain there for ever; I will offer him as a nazirite for all time.' Her husband Elkanah said to her, 'Do what seems best to you, wait until you have weaned him; only—may the Lord establish his word.' So the woman remained and nursed her son, until she weaned him. When she had weaned him, she took him up with her… to the house of the Lord… And she said, '… For this child I prayed; and the Lord has granted me the petition that I made to him. Therefore I have lent him to the Lord; as long as he lives, he is given to the Lord.' …

Samuel was ministering before the Lord, a boy wearing a linen ephod. His mother used to make for him a little robe and take it to him each year, when she went up with her husband to offer the yearly sacrifice. Then Eli would bless Elkanah and his wife, and say, 'May the Lord repay you with children by this woman for the gift that she made to the Lord'; and then they would return to their home.

And the Lord took note of Hannah; she conceived and bore three sons and two daughters. And the boy Samuel grew up in the presence of the Lord.

1 SAMUEL 1:20–28 (ABRIDGED); 1 SAMUEL 2:18–21

The world is shrinking, so we often hear. Journeys that used to take weeks are covered in hours. Distances that used to separate us from friends and loved ones in different countries, or even in different villages, are readily bridged today by air and road, by satellite and e-mail. Our planet has become, as we say, a 'global village'. Everything has shrunk to a distance within the reach of all of us.

But there is a flip-side to this shrinkage. As the world becomes ever 'smaller', so our own minds and hearts are challenged to *expand*, to make space for more and more of its concerns. When the globe was vast, and the next village a day's journey away, all we had to deal with were the concerns of those in our immediate neighbourhood. By and large, what went on in the rest of the world remained a closed book. Now that the world has become so relatively small, the concerns of everyone have opened up to us. It is no longer possible to close our eyes to the issues that affect our fellow human beings in every corner of the globe. Whatever affects any one of us affects all of us.

I love the story of Hannah, not least because it leads me through this process of shrinking and growing—that double dynamic of the human story.

Hannah longs for a child. Her longing is so deep that she takes it to God in prayer. Eventually her prayer is answered and she conceives Samuel. So far, this is just a bit of 'local news'. A woman has conceived a child. It happens all the time—hardly a world-changing matter. No one outside of Hannah's neighbourhood would have known or cared about this minor event.

But the birth of a child is always a life-changing event, certainly for the child and the child's family. Hannah's response is to make this gift-child over to the Lord, who has given him to her in the first place. The child she has longed for above all else, she now gives back to the Lord. The heartache in this decision can only be imagined. But Hannah's story gives us, perhaps, a little insight into the strange process by which the world can shrink, so that it appears totally within our reach, and yet at the same time challenges our minds and hearts to expand to contain it.

In the birth of her son, Hannah, like all new parents, becomes totally focused on the new life in her arms. All creation, it might feel, is gathered here in this one tiny new being, and all her own energies are directed into caring for him. She suckles him and weans him, and then gives him back to the world and to the creator of that world. And then the growing begins! Every year, we learn, she goes back to the temple, taking Samuel a new coat. It would be so easy to forget—amid all the temple rituals—that this is a little human being who will grow out of his coat every year. A mother doesn't forget! She deals with the problem. And we can imagine the little boy bursting out of each outgrown coat, and then losing himself in the new one that, like a school outfit at the start of the new school year, was probably way too big for him.

This incident, tucked away in the history of the people of Israel, reminds me that I too need new mental and spiritual 'clothes' each year. I grow out of my mindsets just as a child grows out of its clothes. Every time a bit more of the world, its people and their concerns come to my attention, my mindset has to grow to respond to the new challenges that come with them. I find that I can rarely respond fully to tomorrow's problems using yesterday's mindsets. Fortunately, God does for us what Hannah does for Samuel. God waits patiently, holding each new coat for us until we are ready to grow into it—which means, of course, that we have to let the outgrown mindset go, a process that isn't always a painless one.

*'His mother used to make for him a little robe
and take it to him each year'*

Look back over any significant 'growth spurts' in your own life, and
remember how it felt to let go of outgrown mindsets in order to be
clothed in a bigger way of looking at things. Is there a change like
this around in your life right now?

*Lord, I know that my mindset is way too small, but I'm afraid
to let go of it. Please ease me into my new and bigger one,
that will give me space to grow. Amen*

Readiness

'Then the kingdom of heaven will be like this. Ten bridesmaids took their lamps and went to meet the bridegroom. Five of them were foolish, and five were wise. When the foolish took their lamps, they took no oil with them; but the wise took flasks of oil with their lamps. As the bridegroom was delayed, all of them became drowsy and slept. But at midnight there was a shout, "Look! Here is the bridegroom! Come out to meet him." Then all those bridesmaids got up and trimmed their lamps. The foolish said to the wise, "Give us some of your oil, for our lamps are going out." But the wise replied, "No! There will not be enough for you and for us; you had better go to the dealers and buy some for yourselves." And while they went to buy it, the bridegroom came, and those who were ready went with him into the wedding banquet; and the door was shut. Later the other bridesmaids came also, saying, "Lord, lord, open to us." But he replied, "Truly I tell you, I do not know you." Keep awake therefore, for you know neither the day nor the hour.'

MATTHEW 25:1–13

To wait in wisdom is to wait in a state of readiness. The very words 'a state of readiness' can fill our hearts with dread, living as we do in such a dangerous world, where 'readiness' is so often equated with the availability of firepower and the machinery of destruction. It conjures up images of 'red alert', where the worst is expected and an atmosphere of fear prevails. This, surely, is not the kind of readiness Jesus is urging in this parable.

I remember a startling encounter with 'readiness' that

happened when I was in my early teens. With a school-friend of my own age, I had been preparing for confirmation. The day came and we walked together to the altar and knelt together to receive the sacrament of confirmation and to make our first holy communion. Not long afterwards, my friend became seriously ill with leukaemia, and died at the age of 15. Amid the shock and disbelief that such a promising young life had been snuffed out so suddenly, I remember our vicar's words to me. 'She was ready to die,' he said. I was appalled. But over time I came to realise that he was right. He had seen something of her soul that had been hidden from me. He had known her with just a little of the knowledge God has of her. And the more I reflected on his words, the more clear it became to me that Madeleine had indeed already been living in a depth of peace that one rarely sees in one so young. She had known, instinctively, how to 'trim her lamp', and there was plenty of oil in the depths of her heart. When the bridegroom arrived for her, she was ready. She followed him gladly, and there was a strange joy amid the sorrow. The reflection of that light has continued to accompany me and often to show me the way through the many years that have intervened.

So what kind of a 'lamp' is it that we are being asked to 'trim'? What does this 'readiness' mean for us at a personal level?

I had the privilege of spending a quiet day once in a lovely old house whose owners use their home as a retreat for others who are seeking the stillness of prayer. They themselves are people who live in that 'state of readiness' that was so characteristic of my friend Madeleine. The lamp of their love is constantly aglow, waiting to leap into a powerful flame when it is needed by someone who has lost themselves in the dark of pain or sorrow or confusion. They say little. They listen deeply. They are simply a loving presence to all comers. So it was that I settled into the room they had lovingly prepared for me, and the first thing I noticed was a little oil lamp and a box of matches. I lit the lamp, and watched the flame burn steadily, but my gaze soon followed the wick down to the oil in the glass base of the lamp. Not for the first time in my life I felt that God was spelling out to my slow mind something that was abundantly obvious, but that I hadn't taken on board in any real way until I saw it embodied in this little lamp: *the wick will only burn at one end if the other end remains dipped in the oil.*

An oil lamp is a powerful parable of 'readiness'. We become ready for closer union with God and with each other to the extent that the base of our 'wick'—the core of our being—remains submerged in the oil. And we become ready to give light in the world to the extent that the visible end of our 'wick' stretches *out* into that world, sharing in all its hardships and concerns. As long as this is the case, the oil of God's presence will rise steadily through our whole being and turn into our own kind of light for the world. If this connection is broken, our light will flicker and fail.

The process is silent and unseen. God rises through our living in ways we cannot perceive or understand. And each of us must find our own way both of staying immersed in the oil and of being present to the concerns of the world. We stay in the oil through the practice of prayer, whatever form that may take. We burn in the world through the nurturing of deep and loving relationships with other people and with all creation, and through our striving for justice and peace. Without the oil of God's constant presence there can be no flame of action in the visible world.

We can't draw this life-giving energy from anywhere but the oil of our own personal relationship with God. There are no 'five wise bridesmaids' sitting alongside who will fill up our lamp from their own supplies. This parable reminds us that it is our own responsibility, as well as our joy, to keep our wicks immersed in God. When we do, the flame will burn in a world that is desperate for light and warmth.

'The wise took flasks of oil with their lamps'

Spend a few moments reflecting on your own life's 'lamp'. In what ways is its flame burning and giving light to the world? Where is the source of that energy? Where is the 'oil'? How do you personally ensure that your 'wick' remains immersed in the 'oil' of God's presence?

> Lord, 'give me oil in my lamp, keep me burning'. Let me live in the readiness that comes from your constant love. Amen

Suffering

Now there was a woman who had been suffering from haemorrhages for twelve years. She had endured much under many physicians, and had spent all that she had; and she was no better, but rather grew worse. She had heard about Jesus, and came up behind him in the crowd and touched his cloak, for she said, 'If I but touch his clothes, I will be made well.' Immediately her haemorrhage stopped; and she felt in her body that she was healed of her disease. Immediately aware that power had gone forth from him, Jesus turned about in the crowd and said, 'Who touched my clothes?' And his disciples said to him, 'You see the crowd pressing in on you; how can you say, "Who touched me?"' He looked all round to see who had done it. But the woman, knowing what had happened to her, came in fear and trembling, fell down before him, and told him the whole truth. He said to her, 'Daughter, your faith has made you well; go in peace, and be healed of your disease.'

MARK 5:25–34

Humanity has struggled through the centuries with the question of suffering. Is it something intrinsically evil that we should do everything to eradicate? Is it something potentially redemptive that takes us deep into the core of our being, in search of healing? Is it something we have to live with—or fight against? Or does the paradox of suffering, perhaps, include elements of all these things?

The woman in today's story has lived for twelve years with a debilitating condition. Her continual haemorrhaging has drained her of all her life energy. It has also rendered her ritually 'unclean' under Jewish law, and condemned her into the role of outcast. But with her last ounce of energy she seeks out Jesus, trusting implicitly that merely to touch the hem of this man's garment will bring her healing.

This story always reminds me of a time in my own life when I was struggling with difficulties that seemed to offer no hope of any improvement. Like the woman in the story, I had invested a lot of time and energy in seeking help, but to no avail. When I recall this experience, I can feel with the woman's desperation. Perhaps you too have memories of being in a place where there seemed to be no hope of an end to a particular kind of suffering you were enduring.

I remember, especially, one morning when I hit a trough. Everything suddenly overwhelmed me in a wave of pain and tears, but at the same time I had been reflecting, somewhere in the depths of my heart, on this story of the woman with the haemorrhage. Somehow, that morning, these two facts came together. All I know is that I fell into a deep sleep through sheer exhaustion, and when I woke I felt deeply refreshed, as though in my sleep I too had touched the hem of the Lord's garment. I share this story only in the hope that it might trigger your own memories of when you have 'touched the Lord's garment' yourself. That touch may have taken any number of forms. It may have been a moment of desperate vocal prayer, or the act of turning to someone else in your need. Jesus can touch us through each other's love. His hands are our hands now, and the hem of our garments can be the hem of his, if we are willing to let him live in us and through us.

But the incident is not quite as straightforward as it appears. Jesus is as deeply affected by the woman's touch as she is herself. He knows that they have encountered each other at the most profound level, and he knows that this encounter needs to be openly acknowledged. There has been an exchange of energy between them—and exchange of her suffering for his strength.

In a moving story by Walter Wangerin, Jesus is described as a 'Ragman', who trundles through the world offering 'new rags for old'. As he meets one suffering person after another, the Ragman takes away the rags of suffering—bloodstained bandages, masks of pain, blankets of despair—and gives the sufferer new clothing. But these are not simply 'healing miracles'. They are acts of exchange, because, while each sufferer is healed and renewed, the Ragman himself takes on their suffering in his own life, until at last, overwhelmed by the weight of the world's pain, he dies alone on a landfill site. The story leads to resurrection, however, on the other side of death, and it holds the implicit call to each of us to live the Ragman's ministry in our own small way. It calls us to engage with the suffering of each other, risking the exposure to pain we would rather avoid, allowing the sufferer to touch the hem of our garment and trusting that God will use the encounter to bring new life. (See Walter Wangerin Jnr, *Ragman and Other Cries of Faith*, Harper and Row, 1984.)

The woman's suffering in today's story becomes her personal gateway to God. If she had not been in pain, she might never have encountered Jesus in the crowd. Through her suffering and her desperate need, she meets him in an intimacy she could never have dared to imagine. That intimacy demands an openness and truthfulness that reveals her in all her vulnerability to herself, to the crowd and to God. It challenges her to say, simply, 'Jesus, take me as I am!'

Our bodies and minds have their own God-given wisdom that tells them when they need to reach out to God for healing and restoration. It is our suffering that brings us to the point of such an encounter. When this happens, our lives engage in the amazing and continuous exchange of God's wholeness for our brokenness, God's love for our pain.

'If I but touch his clothes, I will be made well'

Can you recall any moments in your own life when some personal suffering became too much to bear? Perhaps, in your own way, you reached out then to 'touch the hem of Jesus' garment'. If so, what form did that 'touch' take, and how did God respond? Remember, with gratitude, any human help that was given at that time.

Remembering this experience, be open to the possibility that any pain you may experience in the future, either in body or in mind, is potentially another gateway to God and a new opening to a greater fullness of life in him.

Lord, I would do anything to avoid the pain in my life, and even the pain in other people's lives. Please give me the courage to enter into suffering not just as a place of darkness, but as a gateway of possibility, where I can meet you, touch you and receive your healing love. Amen

Recognition

In those days Mary set out and went with haste to a Judean town in the hill country, where she entered the house of Zechariah and greeted Elizabeth. When Elizabeth heard Mary's greeting, the child leaped in her womb. And Elizabeth was filled with the Holy Spirit and exclaimed with a loud cry, 'Blessed are you among women, and blessed is the fruit of your womb. And why has this happened to me, that the mother of my Lord comes to me? For as soon as I heard the sound of your greeting, the child in my womb leaped for joy. And blessed is she who believed that there would be a fulfilment of what was spoken to her by the Lord.'

LUKE 1:39–45

Yesterday's window opened up into a place of pain and unease—a place where we need to say, 'No! I can't take any more!' but lit by the possibility that our experience of suffering may be God's invitation to us to bring deep-buried issues into the light of God's healing love.

Today's window is a gateway to a different possibility— the possibility of recognising an indestructible truth and knowledge in the core of our being. It is about the swell of joy, the thrill of 'Yes!' that we sometimes experience when something in the ground of our own being has touched something in the ground of another person's being. The resulting resonance is part of God's eternal harmony. We know it, and we long to sing it!

There is a piece of folk wisdom that tells of a person who was asked to look out of a clear glass window and tell of what he saw. 'I see the street,' he said, 'and my fellow human beings going about their business.' The same person was then invited to look into a mirror and tell of what he saw. 'I see myself,' he said. 'I see my own reflection.' The tale goes on to point out that the mirror differs from the window only in its silver coating, and that often it is our own 'silver'— our possessions and wealth, real or merely dreamed of— that cause us to look into the glass pane of life and see only ourselves reflected back.

Mary and Elizabeth certainly do not appear to have been weighed down with 'silver'. Today, as we share in their meeting, we see two women who look through the 'glass' of their encounter and see each other. Even more interestingly, each of them needs the other to remind her of who she really is, so far are they both from being self-obsessed.

I often visit this scene in my prayer and my thoughts. I imagine Mary, in her desperate situation, taking herself off to her older cousin Elizabeth who, she believes, will somehow understand, will accept her condition without raised eyebrows and will give her refuge while she thinks things through. I imagine the look in her eyes as she greets Elizabeth—an expression of reverence for the older woman, who has also been chosen by God to carry a special child— an expression of expectation and trust that Elizabeth will provide the solid basis of wisdom that she so longs for in her new situation. Elizabeth, on the other hand, looks at Mary with the eyes of love and reveres what she sees, in awe that she should be sought out by the mother of her Lord.

And then, that moment when the unborn John leaps in recognition of the unborn Jesus! Even in the womb there is this deep recognition.

In the mirror we recognise ourselves. Through the glass of the window we recognise each other. But in the moment of deepest intimacy, when heart lies open to heart, we recognise God in each other. This is not just a moment shared between two exceptional women, recounted in scripture. It happens every time we are alongside each other with truly open hearts. When this happens, 'deep calls to deep', and we discover that there is resonance with the other person at the core of our being. This 'leap' of the heart towards the heart of the other is the hallmark of real 'soul friendship'.

I recently had the great privilege of meeting a man— another John—already in his 60s, who has spent the last 15 or more years caring tirelessly and lovingly for his ailing and elderly parents. This task has taken over his life, leaving him little time or energy for anything else, yet he has done it with joy. Sadly, I met him at his mother's funeral. She had been bedridden for years, in a nursing home, and the nursing staff were vigorous in their praise of how he had visited her every day, sat vigil with her through many a long night and loved her unstintingly. He phoned me this morning to thank me for going to her funeral! He went on to say how wonderful the staff in the nursing home had been, and how selfless in their care for her. All he could see was the goodness in them. He needed me to hold up the mirror that revealed that same goodness in himself.

It reminded me of Mary and Elizabeth. Each of them could see the goodness in the other. They needed each other to recognise the presence of God in themselves.

May our eyes not rest too long on the mirror of our own reflection, but may our gaze move out, through the window pane, to see the wonder of all that is 'other', beyond our own life's orbit, and to recognise God in the core of that 'other'.

The windows of our Advent calendar now invite us to come closer, not only to look at but to *enter into* what we see. As we move into the days surrounding the birth of Jesus, our Advent journey changes gear as we respond to the heavenly invitation to 'come and see this thing that has come to pass'.

'As soon as I heard your greeting, the child in my womb leapt for joy'

Reflect on any moments in your own life when you have been aware of a deeper recognition of the reality of God coming to birth in another person, and their recognition of the reality of God coming to birth in you. Do you have a 'soul-friend'? If so, you might like to visit him or her, and have a talk about how your journey with God is going.

Lord, please give us the grace to see beyond our own reflection to all that is 'other', the wisdom to recognise you in that 'other', and the courage to enter lovingly into what we see. Amen

22–28 December

Entering the Mystery

As we come closer to the festival of Christmas, we join Joseph and Mary on their journey to Bethlehem and allow them to draw us with them into the very heart of the mystery. This is a journey we are called to join in, not to observe from a safe distance.

- It is a journey that will lead us to a deeper understanding of where we 'belong', and how that 'belonging' calls us into new ways of relating to each other and to God (22 December)
- Jesus is conceived into emptiness—an empty, waiting womb. We reflect on our own awareness of the empty spaces in our lives, and how they can become containers for God's overflowing grace (23 December)
- We share in the stillness of the Holy Night, and seek to meet God in the depths of our own hearts' stillness (24 December)
- God is the 'God of surprises', who gives Godself to us in the surprise of Christmas morning, and in every new surprise that awaits us around the next corner (25 December)
- In the stable at Bethlehem, the light of the world has dawned. To enter into this light is also to see our own

shadows revealed, yet we enter it in trust, knowing that the light is always more powerful than the darkness in which it is kindled (26 December)

- We often 'labour' ourselves, to 'deliver' what we think is a 'happy Christmas'. In the days that follow the feast, let us also rest and, with the Child's mother, ponder in our hearts the wonder that is unfolding for us (27 December)
- And finally, the shadows lengthen over Bethlehem, and the tyrant's sword strikes terror. Yet our woundedness can also become our blessing. The bittersweet birth of God in our hearts will bring both the wounding and the blessing, as we enter the mystery and commit ourselves to carry the light of Christ out into the waiting world (28 December)

Belonging

In those days a decree went out from Emperor Augustus that all the world should be registered. This was the first registration and was taken while Quirinius was governor of Syria. All went to their own towns to be registered. Joseph also went from the town of Nazareth in Galilee to Judea, to the city of David called Bethlehem, because he was descended from the house and family of David. He went to be registered with Mary, to whom he was engaged and who was expecting a child.

LUKE 2:1–5

Now the Lord said to Abram, 'Go from your country and your kindred and your father's house to the land that I will show you. I will make of you a great nation, and I will bless you, and make your name great, so that you will be a blessing.'

GENESIS 12:1–2

As a cat lover I appreciated a cat joke I heard recently: 'A dog has a master,' it said, 'but a cat has staff!'

Having for many years been one of the staff in attendance on one cat after another, I know just how true that is. We can speak of 'dog owners' quite happily, and we know that most dogs are more than happy to 'belong' to their owners. To speak of 'owning' a cat, however, is a nonsense. Cats *choose* to live with you. They don't allow anyone to 'own' them. *They* decide where they 'belong', and to what extent.

Does this have anything to show us about the nature of 'belonging' that today's readings explore?

Joseph, we learn, belongs to Bethlehem, because that is where his forebears are from. He is, as it were, on the electoral register there. And Mary, his betrothed, belongs to him, and becomes obligated to register wherever he belongs. The call to Joseph comes from secular authority and invokes the power to demand that he return to Bethlehem, so that he can be counted in the census.

Abram belongs in Haran, in Mesopotamia. That is the place where his forebears have led him. The call to Abram comes from God, and challenges him to move *away* from his native land, so that the journey to the promised land can begin.

Two different calls, but both in different ways about the question of 'belonging', and both precipitating a world-changing journey.

Probably all of us have a deep desire to belong. Small children accept unquestioningly that they belong to a particular family and place. It gives (or should give) them a sense of safety. Young people tend to find their belonging in their peer group. To fall out of line with one's peers is to risk major insecurity. Adults often satisfy their need to belong by entering into exclusive relationships, and by identifying themselves with the job they do or the groups they associate with. All this is fine and necessary, of course. It gives structure and boundaries to our lives.

But the word 'belong' is a two-edged sword. It can be about the entirely good and necessary sense of being 'at home' in a place, a relationship or a group; or it can be about possession. It begins with 'my house belongs to me', and can move, dangerously, into '*you* belong to me (and must therefore submit to my will)' and 'you belong to our group, and no criticism of that group is allowed'.

Joseph experiences these two different aspects of belonging in quick succession. Through his God-given dream, he has begun to understand that he and Mary belong together in this awesome call to bring God's Son to birth, and he has accepted the responsibility that this belonging implies. Very soon afterwards, he is called to Bethlehem because the authorities there have certain rights of possession over him. The exercise of those rights causes considerable hardship to the embryonic holy family.

'Belonging', in its possessive sense, always seems to limit freedom, forcing us to fit into the mould of the ones who are doing the possessing—making Joseph journey to Bethlehem at the height of Mary's pregnancy, making us conform to another person's demands, making us toe the party line. The one who 'possesses' may use that power wisely or maliciously, but it remains a question of power.

God's view of belonging seems to be more about relationship than possession. It calls us into greater freedom, if we dare to respond. Joseph is called into full and loving relationship with Mary and her unborn child. Abram is called into a fuller relationship with God and God's people. This kind of belonging is not about power, but about a desire to commit ourselves in trust to live in a new kind of relationship. It doesn't compel us—it is something we are invited to choose.

When we make a choice to enter into this radical kind of belonging, we enter upon a journey of mystery. We have no idea, for example, what life will bring when we enter into a committed relationship with another human being. We commit ourselves to belong together through thick and thin. To commit ourselves to follow the promptings of God into the unknown is an even more mysterious undertaking. For Joseph and Mary, as for Abram, this new relationship leads to a journey fraught with risk and hardship, taking them far away from the 'fixed abode' of their earlier securities and certainties.

If we choose to be in personal relationship with God, we may discover that the only place we can really feel we 'belong' is to the journey itself—the journey into the depths of the mystery we call God.

'Go from your country to the land that I will show you'

Is there any 'belonging' of the possessive kind in your life? Does any individual or group have a possessive hold over you? If so, how do you feel about it?

What relationships have you freely chosen, as your places of belonging? What journeys have they led you into? How do you feel about where those journeys are leading?

Lord, to belong to you is to find my home only in the journey that leads into your mystery. Please give me the courage to embrace the challenge of that journey. Amen

Emptiness

While they were there, the time came for her to deliver her child. And she gave birth to her firstborn son and wrapped him in bands of cloth, and laid him in a manger, because there was no room for them in the inn.

LUKE 2:6–7

Now when Jesus saw great crowds around him, he gave orders to go over to the other side. A scribe then approached and said, 'Teacher, I will follow you wherever you go.' And Jesus said to him, 'Foxes have holes, and birds of the air have nests, but the Son of Man has nowhere to lay his head.'

MATTHEW 8:18–20

> *Tremble, O earth, at the presence of the Lord,*
> *at the presence of the God of Jacob,*
> *who turns the rock into a pool of water,*
> *the flint into a spring of water.*
> PSALM 114:7–8

There was a touching little news item not long ago on television about a rabbit who had been rendered homeless because the pregnant family cat had taken over his hutch and set it up as a nursery for her forthcoming litter of kittens. The TV cameras zoomed in to reveal a rather unhappy and bewildered bunny and a very satisfied cat curled up in the hutch, suckling her young family.

The nesting instinct makes itself felt during pregnancy in many different ways. Most mothers-to-be feel a nudge somewhere inside to take some steps to prepare a place for the coming child to be welcomed into the home. Bedrooms are decorated, and cots installed. Soft toys are chosen and tiny baby clothes are laid out in readiness. The instinct is strong. If necessary, the mother-to-be will make great sacrifices to furnish a nest for the child. It is the beginning of a long period of cherishing and protecting the new generation. And Jesus reminds us that this instinct extends through all the natural world. Foxes have holes; birds build nests. Every creature knows, in its own way, how to make empty, neutral space into a home.

Yet when God is born among us, there is no nest. Instead, Mary spends the final weeks of her pregnancy trekking to Bethlehem, jogged and jostled on the rough back of a donkey. The journey that began in trust leads ever more threateningly into the unknown. Will there be anywhere to stay in Bethlehem? Will there be somewhere warm and sheltered to give birth? The questions must have teemed through her mind as they travelled on.

Of course, we know the answer. The answer was 'No!' For God, there was only the most makeshift and temporary of nests—in a manger, not in the living space of the inn, but in the part where the animals were kept. And we, whom Jesus calls his brothers and sisters, can expect no more as we make our journey through life in his company.

And it seems to matter to God that God's Son finds only empty space where there should be 'home'. You may know the story of the little boy who had been chosen to play the part of the innkeeper in the school nativity play. When Mary and Joseph knocked at his door, he felt so sorry for them that he changed the script and said, 'Come on in, you can have my bedroom!' Our hearts want to say that too. And it's easy to say it in the quiet of our prayer or in the exuberant singing of Christmas carols. It's much harder when we meet God in the terrified faces of our nation's 'enemy', or in the hopeless expression of the asylum seeker, or in the young person sleeping in a cardboard box on the high street. Because to say to *them*, 'Come on in, you can have my bedroom' would mean that we would have to move out! We would have to make space for them, by surrendering our own space and risking an unthinkable emptiness.

But the third reading today gives me real hope. God, it reminds us, turns rocks into pools, and flint into fountains. I don't need to search far for the evidence of this fact. Our countryside is full of lakes and ponds, and our hillsides are alive with waterfalls. And these lovely places depend for their very existence on the presence of an empty space where the water can gather, or where the flow of the stream can break through. Emptiness, not fullness, is the secret of these blessings.

When I take these reflections into my own life, I find exactly the same kind of truth. The grace of God has found space in my life in the empty, hollowed-out spaces in my heart, not in the parts of my life that I have managed to fill up with my own 'achievements'. The fountains of God's love have become real and effective where my own defences broke down. My breakdowns became God's breakthroughs.

The hollowing out of these spaces has often been painful and heart-breaking, and I would have avoided it if I had seen it coming. Yet now, in hindsight, I can come to these pools and drink deeply from a strength and a love I could never have imagined possible.

God chose an empty space in which to make a nest for Jesus. God chose a virgin's womb, and then prepared that nest by emptying it even further. Mary and Joseph, who began with nothing, lose even their home base and their security en route to Bethlehem. Yet the more deeply their lives are hollowed out, the more grace can flow into the emptiness—grace that will overflow and flood all the world with God's love.

'There was no room for them in the inn'

When you look back over the most important things that have shaped your life, do you find that they grew out of your own 'fullness' or an inner 'emptiness'? Can you see any 'hollows' in your experience that may well have been carved out of you in pain, but have become containers of grace?

Lord, sometimes all I have to bring you are my empty hollows and the flint of my pain. Fill my emptiness, I beg you, with your love, and break through my hard rock in waterfalls of love, overflowing to your thirsty world. Amen

Stillness

And the Word became flesh and lived among us, and we have seen his glory, the glory as of a father's only son, full of grace and truth.
JOHN 1:14

When peaceful silence lay over all, and night had run half of her swift course, your all-powerful word, O Lord, leaped down from heaven, from the royal throne.
WISDOM 18:14–15 (APOCRYPHA, JB)

It is a cold December night as I walk across the Bornholmer Brücke—a humpbacked bridge that connects the former East Berlin to the former West, arching awkwardly over the inner-city railway lines. The frost is sharp, and a layer of Christmas snow encrusts the streets, squeaking beneath my feet, at −15°C. The moon rides high in the black of the night—a perfect half-moon. The clean lines of its silver hemisphere might have been cut with a knife. Half a moon, and a broken-backed bridge, halfway through the night, at the turning of a year.

The night is vivid for me for other reasons too. For several years I lived in a near-derelict tenement block just the other side of this bridge. I remember how I sometimes walked up to the frontier and watched the bristling guards watching me— how I shielded my eyes against the flare of the searchlights that were combing and roving the no-man's land with predatory malice, demonic mockeries of the silver moonlight.

The city is free now, and this bridge that once divided it

reconnects its severed halves. The streets have calmed down, as the last shopping day before Christmas slips away. There are many people living here now who have no personal memory of the night the Berlin Wall came down. I lived here in the 1960s, when the Wall was new, and sinister, and hated. Passing, then, between East and West across the checkpoint had been as stark and sharp as a knife-cut. I had functioned at that time as a thin and fragile vein, tenuously connecting the severed limbs of the family by virtue of my foreign passport that opened the borders for me, albeit creakingly.

Then half the city had struggled in a bleak darkness, and the other half had teemed in a bright, but garish, commercial light. But now it is different. Some of the buildings from the time of the Wall are still here in the East, but Western culture has rained down its neon lights and satellite dishes and fast food chains over the greyness, like cheap tinsel on a dark, brooding pine tree.

The story of the divided city had been like a long, dark night, running its course not swiftly but interminably and bloodily, a focal point of European history. The bridge's broken back had been an image in iron of a people's broken connections and their aching pain, their own backs arched in impotent anger. None of us then had truly believed we would see the day when the Wall would fall. Everyone believed that it would surely happen sometime, like the second coming, but no one *expected* it. When we woke up each morning, we didn't ever think, 'Maybe *today*?' We adjusted our dreams and our visions to the lack of freedom, peace and justice, instead of adjusting our world to embody our dreams and visions.

The tide turned suddenly, while no one was looking. The wind of change blew up like a freak storm, whipping up our unspoken desires until the collective whisper grew into a rumbling and a roar. 'You call us the People's Republic. But we are the people!' It was a powerful word, wielded without force, springing out of a smothered silence, leaping out of the free spirit of humankind to challenge the darkness. No one who knows this city will ever forget the day that freedom pierced the darkness, like a bolt from the blue, and made the first breach in the Wall that had seemed so permanent. It came so suddenly, so utterly surprisingly, like a baby in a stable, so vulnerable, beneath a cold, shining moon. When night had run half of her swift course…

From a distant clock tower, I hear the stroke of midnight. The world is still journeying through a long, dark night, and there is a long way to go before daybreak as together we labour to bring God to birth in our darkest human situations. But as I stand here, it is the bright half of the moon I see, not the dark side, and it is the stillness that fills my heart, not the heavy hooves of history. I hear a Word more powerful than all our revolutions, yet gentler than a baby's sigh. A Word with the power, and the desire, to leap from mystery into history and turn the world's course away from darkness and into the radiance of God's dream.

'Peaceful silence lay over all'

Take five minutes, today, to be perfectly still. The Christ is born into our hearts' stillness, not just today but every moment. He is the turning point of all our nights. Be still, and know that he is God.

The night has been lonely, Lord, and the way has been long.
Open our eyes tonight to hear your eternal Word, entering
the midnight silence of our human story. Amen

Surprises

In that region there were shepherds living in the fields, keeping watch over their flock by night. Then the angel of the Lord stood before them, and the glory of the Lord shone around them, and they were terrified. But the angel said to them, 'Do not be afraid; for see—I am bringing you good news of great joy for all the people: to you is born this day in the city of David a Saviour, who is the Messiah, the Lord. This will be a sign for you: you will find a child wrapped in bands of cloth and lying in a manger.' And suddenly there was with the angel a multitude of the heavenly host, praising God and saying, 'Glory to God in the highest heaven, and on earth peace among those whom he favours!'

When the angels had left them and gone into heaven, the shepherds said to one another, 'Let us go now to Bethlehem and see this thing that has taken place, which the Lord has made known to us.' So they went with haste and found Mary and Joseph, and the child lying in the manger. When they saw this, they made known what had been told them about this child; and all who heard it were amazed at what the shepherds told them.

LUKE 2:8–18

The company that could manufacture 'joy', and market it in person-sized packages, would sweep the board. Many have tried, and all have failed. At this time of the year especially, everyone is searching for the magic ingredient that will make this day *joyful*. During the past few weeks, or even months, we have been inundated by all the permutations on offer. It's very hard to escape the conclusion that if we spend enough money, consume enough food and drink and arrange for the right combination of people to share our Christmas table, all will be well.

Yet, to our cost, we know that it isn't always so. Christmas sees the highest prevalence of suicide in the year. Many, many people simply dread the approach of the 'festive season', and even those who do have families and friends with whom to share the festivities sometimes find, on Boxing Day, that they are tense and exhausted and feel that they simply 'tried too hard' and are relieved that 'it's all over for another year'.

Yet this is the day, above all, when God gives joy to the world! What was it that the shepherds understood, but that eludes us today? What are we missing? We, who try so very hard, and with genuine good will, to make Christmas a special day, all too often miss out on the joy it is supposed to bring. The shepherds weren't trying at all. For them it was just another night on the hillside, getting on with their routine work. The whole thing took them completely by *surprise*.

It begins with a surprise visit! The last thing the shepherds were expecting on a cold night out on the hillside was a visit from the heavenly hosts. Surprise visits are a mixed blessing at the best of times, and perhaps especially at Christmas. They are so much a part of what Christmas is about, and, with our lips at least, we welcome them. 'Why don't you drop round for a drink?' we invite the neighbours genially, but secretly hope they will come at the 'right' time, and not outstay their welcome. The angels didn't wait to be invited. The news they had was so momentous that there was no way it could wait until the invitation cards had been printed. And it called forth a response in the shepherds that went a good deal further than a mince pie and a cup of tea. Perhaps because they were themselves at the bottom of the social heap, with no image to defend, they seem to have been amazingly open to the angels' message, once they had overcome their initial shock—so open that they immediately set off to make a surprise visit themselves, to the little family in Bethlehem.

We can only imagine the reaction of Mary and Joseph to the sudden arrival of these unexpected guests! No chance to clean up the stable or bake a cake. 'You'll have to take us as you find us!' we sometimes warn our would-be guests, which, for me at least, is usually an excuse for being too lazy to clean the house up. God says the same, but from a higher motive. 'Come and look for me where you least expect me, and then be prepared to take me as you find me!' Where will we find God this Christmas? Certainly in the hospitality of our friends. But perhaps, more visibly and powerfully, in the faces of those who have no home, no friends, no resources behind which to hide their extreme vulnerability. A surprise visit to such a person would perhaps surprise us with the warmth it would generate.

Surprises are the very essence of Christmas morning. All those gifts we have carefully concealed are joyfully unwrapped. Those with children will be bombarded today with demands to 'Look!' and to join in with the new games, admire the new doll, share in the joy. Surprises are for sharing. The bigger the surprise, the less it can be contained. And all our unwrapping and our sharing is just a faint reflection of God's own great act of unwrapping Godself, to reveal a helpless baby in the arms of two inexperienced parents. It was the mother and father of all surprises. No wonder the shepherds ran off to tell everyone they met about the amazing events of an 'ordinary' night.

'All who heard it were amazed'

The vulnerable baby who is God's own self has countless siblings. Some of them live in your neighbourhood. You will recognise them because they are a gift that comes unwrapped, with the eyes of need looking straight into your own—a single parent, a bewildered immigrant, a lonely pensioner. Why not plan to surprise one of them with a touch of God's love this Christmas season. You might be surprised at the results!

Lord, your gift to us of your very self still lies, unwrapped,
in the forgotten corners of our world. Give us, today, the joy of
rediscovering your presence in the presence of each other. Amen

Light

In the beginning was the Word,
and the Word was with God,
and the Word was God.
He was in the beginning with God.
All things came into being through him,
and without him not one thing came into being.
What has come into being in him was life,
and the life was the light of all people.
The light shines in the darkness,
and the darkness did not overcome it…
The true light, which enlightens everyone,
was coming into the world.
He was in the world, and the world came into being through him;
yet the world did not know him.
He came to what was his own,
and his own people did not accept him.
But to all who received him,
who believed in his name,
he gave power to become children of God.
JOHN 1:1–5, 9–12

When our daughter was born, one of the first difficulties we encountered was the problem of light. To make sure that she would always experience the presence of a gentle, comforting light if she awoke during the night, we installed a little lamp close to the nursery door. It also meant that if she cried we could grope our way to her even in a half-asleep state.

However, visits to a newborn baby in the night can be frequent, and can take a heavy toll on the parents' mental and physical well-being. One of the side-effects of surviving on a meagre ration of sleep is that the eyes start to burn. Even the little nursery light, we soon discovered, burned our eyes, especially after the third or fourth unscheduled awakening during the night. So we went to the local electrical shop to ask whether they had any bulbs lower than 15 watts!

It's strange that light that is so needful for growth and life can also be so hurtful when we are unprepared for it.

The beautiful prologue to St John's Gospel speaks of how God's word first brings life into being, and we can almost picture the dawn of creation in his description of a life that springs from God's word and brings light into a dark void. Such immensity lies beyond our imagination, but we can rediscover the awesomeness of this first creating word simply by noticing the gradual growth of something as tiny as a seed. In the winter season the seeds are deep in the darkness of the earth, yet as winter gradually releases its grip, they begin to respond to a light they cannot yet perceive. Deep in the earth they begin to grow. As the strength of daylight increases, and spring approaches, they will eventually break the surface of the soil and grow to become the plants and flowers we recognise and love.

If they could talk, they would perhaps tell us of the joy and comfort they discover in the gentle light of spring, much as, we hope, our little daughter found comfort in the nursery lamp. But the light increases with every passing day. Summer comes and the flowers are exposed to a light with the power to open up those soft petals to an unpredictable exposure. There will be the joy of blossoming and pollination, but also the fierce rays of sunlight that will eventually wither the flower and release the seeds of next year's growth. Every new life likewise faces the light that brings joy, and the light that burns and exposes. Our own lives are no exception.

But we can be so fearful of the light that exposes that we try to hide away from the light that brings life and growth. The seed of God falls into the darkness of our hearts and grows, but the darkness in which it grows feels threatened by it and seeks to suppress or even destroy it, for, as T.S. Eliot says, 'humankind cannot bear too much reality'.

And so the very light that we long for in the hours of our darkness is the same light that we want to dim down because it burns our hearts too much. Perhaps we fear that God's candle in our nursery might become the fierce beam of the interrogator's light, exposing all our darkness. But what if this light, whose glare we so dread, were the beam of the surgeon's light, searching out our need for healing? What if it were the light that releases all our fruitfulness, even as it withers our petals?

But God's light is gentle. For most of us it will grow like the light of springtime, coaxing us out of our darkness. It begins with the 15 watt bulb, as the desire for life and for God gradually awakens in us, and it takes us steadily forward until we are ready for a stronger beam. Let us not say 'No' in fear to what our hearts most desire, for to dim down God's light in our hearts is to subdue life itself.

> 'The light shines in the darkness,
> and darkness did not overcome it'

In a quiet moment, after dark, switch off all the lights and light a candle. What happens to the darkness as soon as you light the candle? What happens to the candlelight? Does the darkness put it out?

Now apply the same logic to any situation in your own life that feels 'dark'. Is there anything you can do, however small, to 'light a candle' in that dark situation—perhaps a calm conversation, a letter, a gesture of reconciliation, a word of challenge? Can you trust that such a candle will also have more power than all the darkness around it?

Lord, I bring you the darkest place in my experience right now, and I ask you to steady my hand as, together, we light a candle that will banish the power of darkness for ever. Amen

Resting

At that time Jesus said, 'I thank you, Father, Lord of heaven and earth, because you have hidden these things from the wise and intelligent and have revealed them to infants; yes, Father, for such was your gracious will. All things have been handed over to me by my Father; and no one knows the Son except the Father, and no one knows the Father except the Son and anyone to whom the Son chooses to reveal him.

'Come to me, all you that are weary and are carrying heavy burdens, and I will give you rest. Take my yoke upon you, and learn from me; for I am gentle and humble in heart, and you will find rest for your souls. For my yoke is easy, and my burden is light.'
MATTHEW 11:25–30

But Mary treasured all these words and pondered them in her heart. The shepherds returned, glorifying and praising God for all they had heard and seen, as it had been told them.
LUKE 2:19–20

The festivities are over, and perhaps we are back to cold turkey. For many of us, a rest is called for after a strenuous few days. For the new parents in Bethlehem, any rest they might have been able to find after the events of the weeks leading up to the birth of Jesus was to be short-lived, but for today, let's join them in the calm of the stable-lodgings. Their son was to become the one who would promise to give them—and us— *rest* for our souls. He was the one who would teach us all that God reveals the secrets of God's mystery to children and to the unlettered, more easily than to those who have the degrees and the certificates. But for today, we find him simply lying in his mother's arms. And we find his parents simply resting in their joy that he has come into the world.

In our more 'advanced' world, such rest might well have been denied to Mary in the name of medical progress. My own 'recovery time' after a hospital confinement was one long round of doing whatever was on the hospital's agenda at any given time. It began at six in the morning and there was no respite until night—except, that is, at visiting time. When the visitors showed up at the doors, we were hastily shunted into bed, where we were supposed to appear serene and untroubled. I'm not sure whether the hospital got extra Brownie points for presenting such a placid set of new mothers to the eyes of the anxious visitors. I only know that I didn't get a moment's rest until I arrived home again. And it was then that nature compelled me, through sheer exhaustion, to spend quality time doing nothing other than simply sitting with my daughter in my arms, letting her be, and learning how to 'be' myself.

I pondered deeply during those times, through daytime and night-time feeds, watching her sleep or waiting for her to awaken. I thought about the world she would grow up into, the person she would become, and what *really* mattered to me. But most of all, I enjoyed those times. With hindsight I can say that I felt closer to the mystery of God, holding this little child, than I had ever come in long years of studying and trying to work things out.

How, I wonder, did we ever learn the things that are most important to us? I suggest that we learned a lot of them just by being still, sometimes alone, sometimes in another person's embrace, perhaps in the dependency of childhood, perhaps in a time when our own strength gave out and we were forced into passivity. We learn to love by being loved. We learn to trust when our needs are cared for by another. We learn courage and resilience when we come against the hard rock and are compelled to rely on resources deeper than our own. We learn life skills by watching another at work. We learn to listen by being listened to, to be tolerant by being tolerated ourselves. So much of what matters most in life we learn simply by watching, gazing, resting in another's arms; and we learn much of this long before we are old enough to realise that there *is* anything to learn.

In Britain we use the term 'reception class' to describe the first class at school for the new beginners. Because we tend to believe that we, the adults, the 'wise and the learned', are the ones who have everything to impart to the young, we think of it as the class where *we* 'receive' these five-year-olds into the world of learning. If we could see with God's eyes, we would surely realise that it is the children who are doing the receiving, because they are so receptive. They are receiving the seeds of their own stories just by listening to the world's stories. They are perfectly willing to drop everything just to watch a beetle cross the floor. The clock, mercifully, hasn't yet caught up with them, and they are wide open to everything that creation is waiting to reveal to them. However active their minds and bodies may be, their souls are still 'at rest'.

I spend a great deal of my time running around like a headless chicken, trying to 'do' things. When I'm not busy 'doing', I'm preparing for the next thing that has to be done. It all feels so important, but when I recall those early days when I had nothing to do but hold my child and watch her grow, I know that *that* was my life's most important learning curve.

'Mary treasured all these words and pondered them in her heart'

Take some quality time today just to 'be'. Spend a little while watching, gazing, pondering. If there is a child around, or if you have a pet, watch them and let the experience go deep into your heart, or simply be present to the wonder of some aspect of the natural world. Let it connect to other times in your life when you have stopped 'doing' for a while, and entered the real world of learning, where the mystery of God has opened up to you and taught you something of eternal importance.

Lord, may I find a way today to make it a little easier
for someone close to me to take a rest? And then, Lord,
may I rest too? Amen

Blessing

The Lord spoke to Moses, saying: 'Speak to Aaron and his sons, saying, "Thus you shall bless the Israelites: You shall say to them,

The Lord bless you and keep you;
the Lord make his face to shine upon you, and be gracious to you;
the Lord lift up his countenance upon you, and give you peace."

So they shall put my name on the Israelites, and I will bless them.'
NUMBERS 6:22–27

When Herod saw that he had been tricked by the wise men, he was infuriated, and he sent and killed all the children in and around Bethlehem who were two years old or under, according to the time that he had learned from the wise men. Then was fulfilled what had been spoken through the prophet Jeremiah:

'A voice was heard in Ramah,
wailing and loud lamentation,
Rachel weeping for her children;
she refused to be consoled, because they are no more.'
MATTHEW 2:16–18

Soon after the 'Velvet Revolution' that freed the Czech Republic from totalitarian rule, during the historic collapse of East European communism in 1989, I was visiting friends in Prague. They were eager to show me the sights of this beautiful city but, having lived there all their lives and shared personally in its sufferings and struggle, they were able to show me places that lay well off the tourist beat.

In one such place, my hostess drew my attention to a dark corner of a nondescript road, and tried, in imperfect English, to explain why this spot was significant. I gathered that there had been some kind of student uprising there, but I couldn't work out, from what she was telling me, how it had ended.

'The students staged a protest against the regime here,' she told me, 'and many of them were blessed.'

I couldn't make any sense of this. The idea of some priest turning up in the middle of a student riot in a communist country to 'bless' its victims seemed bizarre. But no amount of questioning or explanation was able to shed any light upon the matter. We had to leave it as one of life's unsolved mysteries, and accept the linguistic frustrations.

It was only when I was lying in bed that night, still thinking about this strange incident and the 'blessing' that it suddenly occurred to me that my hostess, who spoke several foreign languages, always chose to use French if she could, as this was her preferred second language. And the French word *blesser* means 'to wound'. All became clear in an instant. The student riot had been violently put down, and many of the students had been *wounded*!

Since then I have often wondered about the unintended connection that was made that day in my mind between 'blessing' and 'woundedness'. The child who is born in Bethlehem brings God's eternal blessing to a broken world, yet within a very short time of his birth an atrocity is perpetrated that makes our blood run cold, even at this distance in time. There is a deadly kinship between the massacre of the infants of Bethlehem and the appalling acts of terrorism and 'ethnic cleansing' that stalk our world today. The birth of the child who brings blessing also provokes terrible violence. The wounded world strikes back against God's blessing, and, 33 years later, only the violent death of that same blessed child will turn curse back into blessing.

The massacre at Bethlehem is a stark reminder that this event is not just a cosy nativity scene, where a smiling baby lies on a bed of clean straw, radiant in the starlight. This smiling baby is a *saviour*. He is a saviour because that, above all, is what the world needs. And he is a saviour who will save and bless us not by an act of transcendent power, but by surrendering himself to the very woundedness he comes to heal.

And what of our own woundedness? Can it ever be a blessing? History certainly records many cases of individuals who have found what really mattered to them when they were laid low by injury or illness. There is a folk story about a tribe of people in times gone by who spent all their time and energy searching for the 'holy mountain'. They would run around in circles, bumping into one another in their eagerness to find their goal. But the only ones who ever found it were those who fell over in all the hustle and bustle. Then, lying helpless on their backs, they would look up in their great need and see what their healthy brothers and sisters were persistently missing—the holy mountain!

When I look back over the years of my life, with their successes and their disasters, I know for sure that it has been the disasters that have drawn me closer to God. When I was prone and helpless, I had no option but to acknowledge how much I needed help, to look up and, through my tears, to see God's face looking down, blessing me and keeping me, letting a holy radiance shine on me, bringing me peace.

'The Lord bless you and keep you'

Remember a time in your own life when you have been wounded, either physically or emotionally. With hindsight, can you see how any blessing flowed from that woundedness? How did that blessing take shape in your life, helping you to grow or changing your attitude in any way?

Bring your memories into the stillness of prayer, and for a few minutes do absolutely nothing but sit in the presence of God, letting the warmth of divine love shine through your whole being, like the warmth of a sunlit dawn, bringing you new life.

Lord, the light of your blessing reveals our scars. May our scars lead us into a deeper understanding of your blessing. Amen

29 December–6 January

Windows Become Doors

The supermarkets are stocking up again for the next big shopping spree before New Year. Is Christmas 'over for another year', or is it just beginning? Giving birth to a child is one thing, but bringing that child up to maturity is quite another. It is a long-term commitment—a huge challenge and a great joy. The Christ-child is born in our hearts. How are we going to make this event a reality in our everyday living? At this point in our journey, the windows of our Advent calendar turn into doors, through which we are called out to the waiting world, to turn our believing into loving service.

- Mary and Joseph bring the infant Jesus to the temple, to consecrate him to God, and we join them in listening to the words of Simeon, who had been waiting in patience and in trust for this moment (29 December). He opens the first door for us, and challenges us to walk through into the world Christ has come to save, risking the sword, trusting the grace.
- We allow Jesus to commission us for the onward journey (30 December)
- We receive his anointing, healing our brokenness and marking us out as ones who serve (31 December)

- The onward journey is a journey into transformation— of ourselves and of our world. This transformation is possible only if we are willing to pass through the narrow ways of difficulty and surrender (1 January)
- It is also a journey into freedom. Dare we risk God's liberating power in our lives? (2 January)
- As we journey on, we learn to look for, and to find, God's unfailing nourishment along the way and to drink life-giving water from the unfailing Source of all our energy (3 January)
- Our energy for the journey depends on our staying always rooted in Christ, the vine, and resisting the pervasive human temptation to live by our own strength (4 January)
- The Christmas season is coming to a close, and the postal rush is over, but we ourselves are 'letters of Christ', sent out into the world, carrying his love (5 January)
- Finally, like the Magi, we return to the place we came from, but by a different route. We return to where we belong, but we are changed by the journey and we carry the seeds of ongoing change and growth with us. On 6 January we celebrate the coming of the good news to the whole world, far beyond the land of the nativity.

We have looked into the lighted windows of God's guidance, wisdom and love. We have entered into the mystery of his coming to birth, and we are sent back to make his kingdom a reality in our own place and time.

Revealing

When the time came for their purification according to the law of Moses, they brought [Jesus] up to Jerusalem to present him to the Lord (as it is written in the law of the Lord, 'Every firstborn male shall be designated as holy to the Lord'), and they offered a sacrifice according to what is stated in the law of the Lord, 'a pair of turtle-doves or two young pigeons'.

Now there was a man in Jerusalem whose name was Simeon; this man was righteous and devout, looking forward to the consolation of Israel, and the Holy Spirit rested on him. It had been revealed to him by the Holy Spirit that he would not see death before he had seen the Lord's Messiah. Guided by the Spirit, Simeon came into the temple; and when the parents brought in the child Jesus, to do for him what was customary under the law, Simeon took him in his arms and praised God, saying,

> *'Master, now you are dismissing your servant in peace,*
> *according to your word;*
> *for my eyes have seen your salvation,*
> *which you have prepared in the presence of all peoples,*
> *a light for revelation to the Gentiles*
> *and for glory to your people Israel.'*

And the child's father and mother were amazed at what was being said about him. Then Simeon blessed them and said to his mother Mary, 'This child is destined for the falling and the rising of many in Israel, and to be a sign that will be opposed so that the inner thoughts of many will be revealed—and a sword will pierce your own soul too.'

LUKE 2:22–35

Simeon's words became imprinted upon my mind at a very early age. I was in the choir of the local parish church as a young schoolgirl, and every Sunday we would sing the words of the Nunc Dimittis during Evensong. I loved the words even then. They brought Sunday to the right kind of close, and seemed to bless us on our way into the week ahead.

During these final few days with our Advent calendar, the direction changes. We have allowed its windows to lead us closer and closer to the mystery of God-with-us, and to share something of the joy and the blessing of the nativity, but now Simeon reminds us that we are being sent out, back into the world, carrying with us something of the starlight. Simeon reminds God that it's OK for God to 'let him go', now that he has seen the promised child. What about ourselves? We too, each in our own way, have seen the light of Bethlehem. Is it OK for God to 'let us go'? Are we ready, as Simeon was, to take the next step? For him it was the final passage from mortal to immortal life. For us it is the passage into a new year, full of unknown challenges.

Notice that there are no guarantees! The fact that we have known the touch of God upon our lives is not an insurance policy against anything the world might throw at us in the year ahead. Simeon is under no illusion about what the coming of this child is going to mean. Things are going to get worse, it seems, before they get better. The events of the first Christmas are going to turn the world upside-down, attract opposition and bring deep personal anguish to those who know the child and love him, starting with his mother. The outlook that Simeon describes is not, on the surface, very appealing. We could be forgiven for saying, 'Thank you, but we'll leave things as they are.'

So what keeps us with it? Why do we keep on believing, and seeking to live out our Christian faith, when the prognosis is that we will be challenged to journey through heartbreak as well as through joy?

Perhaps Simeon's encounter with the newborn Christ gives us a clue. For me, this clue lies in the words, 'My eyes have seen your salvation.' My guess is that, for most of us, the reason we keep on travelling the way of Christ is because in some form or other, at some point in our lives, we have *known* in our own personal experience what it means to feel God's touch upon us. This kind of knowledge doesn't lodge in our heads, but in our hearts and in our gut. We know for ever what we have ever known, however fleetingly, of how we, individually and uniquely, have encountered God. Such knowledge can never be negated or argued away. Even if all the outer wrappings of our faith—the creeds and doctrines, the words and rituals—were to disappear or be discredited, no one ever could wipe out that deep inner knowledge we possess, that in our own way we too have seen some glimpse of the reality of God, and it has made a life-changing difference to us.

Of course, we don't want the sword to pierce our hearts, laying bare our secret thoughts, yet, paradoxically, this is also what we deeply desire, if this is the way in which the kingdom of Christ is coming into being in our world.

'My eyes have seen your salvation'

The direction has turned, and now, having been so deeply drawn into the mystery of God incarnate, we are sent out to live what we have seen and known. The sending-out is rooted for each of us in that personal way in which God has revealed the sacred mystery to our own hearts. Spend a little while reflecting on how God has revealed Godself to *you*. The revealing may have happened in big turning points, or just in tiny glimpses of something eternal. What is it in your own spiritual experience that keeps you travelling this way? In what personal way do you feel able to say, with Simeon, 'My eyes have seen something of your reality, Lord. Now you can let me go, to live out that vision, because I shall never again lose what my heart *knows*'?

Lord, please open my eyes, every new day, to see the ways your love is touching my life, then send me forward into tomorrow, to make this love incarnate in your world. Amen

Commissioning

Then Jesus, filled with the power of the Spirit, returned to Galilee, and a report about him spread through all the surrounding country. He began to teach in their synagogues and was praised by everyone.

When he came to Nazareth, where he had been brought up, he went to the synagogue on the sabbath day, as was his custom. He stood up to read, and the scroll of the prophet Isaiah was given to him. He unrolled the scroll and found the place where it was written:

> 'The Spirit of the Lord is upon me,
> because he has anointed me
> to bring good news to the poor.
> He has sent me to proclaim release to the captives
> and recovery of sight to the blind,
> to let the oppressed go free,
> to proclaim the year of the Lord's favour.'

And he rolled up the scroll, gave it back to the attendant, and sat down. The eyes of all in the synagogue were fixed on him. Then he began to say to them, 'Today this scripture has been fulfilled in your hearing.'

LUKE 4:14–21

Every so often, I find myself in a library that houses thousands of theological books. I cast my eyes along the shelves and run my fingers across the leather spines of these imposing volumes, but, deep inside, my heart shrinks and recoils. Can my believing depend on all this stuff? What hope for normal mortals if the brightest brains of the ages have needed miles of shelf space to explore the complexities of what 'faith' means?

The incident described in today's reading dispels those fears totally. In just a single sentence, Jesus tells us all we need to know about the mission we are being invited to engage in.

It's about touching people's lives with hope and encouragement, and giving them real reason to want to go on living, though their world feels dark and hopeless.

It's about speaking the word that gives freedom—freedom to be real, to speak from the heart, to go beyond the fear, to risk breaking out of the old, outgrown moulds that society and 'religion' can set us into.

It's about discovering a deeper layer of vision—of insight— in situations where we can't see our hands in front of us for the fog of bewilderment and confusion.

It's about searching for ways to release ourselves and each other from the oppressions of the 21st century—whether they are the oppressions of political tyranny or poverty and injustice, or the oppression of stress and burnout in a world that just won't wait for us to catch up.

And it's about declaring the truth we know in our hearts, that God (and not the power of the market) is the bottom line of everything we call life—that there is a centre of gravity beyond ourselves that holds us in being.

We see 'mission statements' everywhere around us these days, in the boardrooms of multi-national companies and at the entrance to the supermarket! We may or may not be impressed by what we see there, but in today's reading we hear Jesus' own 'mission statement'. It's simple. It's practical. And it's about relationship with God and with each other. We don't need a degree to understand it, but we do need a grain of humility to try to live it. It calls us to keep our focus firmly on God and on each other in everything we do, and to preface all our decisions and reactions with the question, 'How does this relate to God's mission and my role in it? What is the more Christ-like thing to do next in this particular situation?'

If I let my imagination run free for a moment, I can almost see Jesus standing up in that theology library, much as he did in the synagogue. I can see him looking with the eyes of wisdom and of love through all those books—all the striving of human minds to find the truth—and spelling out again the simplicity, and the challenging profundity, of the call to be Christ-like in our own circumstances and our own generation. I can hear him distilling into a single sentence all that really matters out of all our searching, and turning to each one of us with the words: 'This mission is being fulfilled right now, right where you are, in ways that make a difference to the real world, and you have a role to play in its fulfilment.'

Jesus, we learn, returned to Galilee, to the place where he had been brought up. He proclaimed God's love among the people who had grown up with him, gone to school with him, played in the streets with him. He made God's love incarnate in his generation, for all generations; on his home ground, but for all the earth. When he speaks in his mission statement of the words being fulfilled 'today', he means this year, this week, this moment. When he speaks in Nazareth, he speaks in our country, our town, our street. When he speaks, he asks us first to listen and then to go out and live his words in the place where we find ourselves.

We are co-missioners with Christ and for Christ. We are commissioned by him to make his life and his values incarnate in our day.

'This scripture has been fulfilled in your hearing'

Take a moment to read through and reflect on the points Jesus mentions in his 'mission statement': to bring good news to the afflicted; to set the captives free; to give sight to the blind; to release those who are oppressed, to proclaim God's love in our own way and our own lives.

Notice any one of these points that speaks to your heart especially.

When has God done this for you, probably through the agency of another person?

How might God be inviting you to use your own experience, and the power of the Spirit, to do the same for someone else?

> *Lord, let your mission live on in me—not in what I know,*
> *or even just in what I do, but in who I am, in you. Amen*

Anointing

One of the Pharisees asked Jesus to eat with him, and he went into the Pharisee's house and took his place at the table. And a woman in the city, who was a sinner, having learned that he was eating in the Pharisee's house, brought an alabaster jar of ointment. She stood behind him at his feet, weeping, and began to bathe his feet with her tears and to dry them with her hair. Then she continued kissing his feet and anointing them with the ointment. Now when the Pharisee who had invited him saw it, he said to himself, 'If this man were a prophet, he would have known who and what kind of woman this is who is touching him—that she is a sinner.' Jesus spoke up and said to him, 'Simon, I have something to say to you.' 'Teacher,' he replied, 'speak.'

'A certain creditor had two debtors; one owed five hundred denarii, and the other fifty. When they could not pay, he cancelled the debts for both of them. Now which of them will love him more?' Simon answered, 'I suppose the one for whom he cancelled the greater debt.' And Jesus said to him, 'You have judged rightly.' Then turning towards the woman, he said to Simon, 'Do you see this woman? I entered your house; you gave me no water for my feet, but she has bathed my feet with her tears and dried them with her hair. You gave me no kiss, but from the time I came in she has not stopped kissing my feet. You did not anoint my head with oil, but she has anointed my feet with ointment. Therefore, I tell you, her sins, which were many, have been forgiven; hence she has shown great love. But the one to whom little is forgiven, loves little.' Then he said to her, 'Your sins are forgiven.' But those who were at the table with him

began to say among themselves, 'Who is this who even forgives sins?'
And he said to the woman, 'Your faith has saved you; go in peace.'
LUKE 7:36–50

I am old enough to remember a coronation. It alarms me to recall that it was well over half a century ago! At the time, I was a little girl in primary school, and I can vividly remember being considerably more impressed by the prospect of a day off school than by the pomp and ceremony being displayed on the (then quite rare) television screens. We celebrated that day as a family by making the trek to my grandmother's home in the Lincolnshire countryside. The reason probably had a lot to do with the fact that she possessed one of those rare televisions, and our elders thought it would make a good excuse for a family reunion. I can't even say that I remember seeing much of the proceedings, as no doubt we were supposed to do. But I do remember an exciting day playing with my young cousins in and out of the dykes and hedgerows that characterise that part of the country.

Nevertheless, it's impossible to grow up in a monarchy (even a democratic one) without being aware of the ceremony of the anointing of a crowned head of state. The anointing that takes place in a coronation is an anointing for service, and, even as a child, I do remember being moved by the pictures of a very young woman making solemn and heartfelt promises to serve a nation to the best of her ability. There is something very sacred about the act of anointing. It has been hallowed through all the ages as a symbol of sending out a person to live a life of service for others.

If we are to be sent out into the world to serve others as God has taught us through the life of Jesus, we too will be 'anointed' for the task. But we won't go to that anointing in a golden coach, nor will our commissioning be sealed with orb and sceptre. If the One we follow is any guide of what to expect, the crown will be of thorns, not of gold, and the symbols of power will become icons of helplessness.

That is why today's story of the unruly intruder into the Pharisees' dinner party appeals to me so much, as a more realistic picture of an 'anointing'. There is a 'demon' inside me who revels in this scene and the social disruption it must have caused. The vision of the good and worthy Pharisees, pillars of society, having their aperitifs and hors d'oeuvres interrupted by a woman from the streets sets the scene wonderfully for all that Jesus is going to teach them. This woman has known the touch of Jesus upon her life. The love he has inspired in her is like a bright ball of light that in turn reveals the deep, dark shadows across her life. She brings both of these things—the love and the shame—and anoints Jesus there and then with both tenderness and tears.

Jesus turns the shock-horror reaction of his hosts on its head by reminding them that the measure of our love for him is a reflection not of our worthiness, but of our *need*. We overflow with love when we recognise just how much his touch has healed in us, and how desperately we needed that touch. Our response remains politely lukewarm if we imagine that we are making out quite well on our own, though we might occasionally invite him to share an evening with us.

In her own way, this woman is anointing Jesus for the suffering that lies ahead, but, paradoxically, he is also anointing her, to love and serve her brothers and sisters with that warm river of love that his touch has opened up in her heart. He asks no less of us.

'She has bathed my feet with her tears and dried them with her hair'

The woman in this scene anoints Jesus with love and with tears that both flow out of the emptiness and the brokenness within her. Take a moment to go into the depths of your own emptiness and brokenness. Don't be afraid to do so, because Jesus himself prays with you, and carries you to the darkest recesses of your heart. In that awareness of utter need, 'anoint' him in your own way, either with words or in silence.

Lord, so often I keep you at a safe distance, inviting you into my life only on my own terms. Please unstop the cork of my heart, and free me to pour out my deepest longings for your love, even when they carry me beyond the limits of my own control. Amen

Transforming

See, I am going to bring them forth from the land of the north,
and gather them from the farthest parts of the earth,
among them the blind and the lame,
those with child and those in labour, together;
a great company, they shall return here.
With weeping they shall come,
and with consolations I will lead them back,
I will let them walk by brooks of water,
in a straight path in which they shall not stumble;
for I have become a father to Israel,
and Ephraim is my firstborn…

They shall come and sing aloud on the height of Zion,
and they shall be radiant over the goodness of the Lord,
over the grain, the wine, and the oil,
and over the young of the flock and the herd;
their life shall become like a watered garden,
and they shall never languish again.
Then shall the young women rejoice in the dance,
and the young men and the old shall be merry.
I will turn their mourning into joy,
I will comfort them, and give them gladness for sorrow.
JEREMIAH 31:8–9, 12–13

'Very truly, I tell you, you will weep and mourn, but the world will rejoice; you will have pain, but your pain will turn into joy. When a woman is in labour, she has pain, because her hour has come. But when her child is born, she no longer remembers the anguish

because of the joy of having brought a human being into the world. So you have pain now; but I will see you again, and your hearts will rejoice, and no one will take your joy from you.'
JOHN 16:20–22

One of my most cherished and abiding memories of childhood is of my mother sitting beside the fire each evening, working patiently at her embroidery. It was always a source of amazement to my teachers at school, when they tried to teach me to sew, that such an incompetent child could have sprung from such a gifted mother. And she really was talented. She loved her work, and rejoiced in the beauty that came forth from her needle. Yet the gift was only discovered through need. When my father lost his job and became ill, she had no choice but to look for a way to earn our bread, and she turned to embroidery as her way of keeping our heads above water. When I think of the long, long hours she spent over her work, and the very meagre payments she received, I marvel at her patience. But even more than that, I can see how this whole process became, for us, one of God's transforming acts. And the needle gives me a clue as to how God sometimes does his transforming.

What turns a single length of thread into a part of a beautiful piece of embroidery? What turns the broken threads of our own experience into living strands of a new creation? When I remember my mother, one answer seems to crystallise before me—'the eye of the needle'. I have watched my mother thread her needle thousands of times. I have seen the coloured embroidery silks being cut off and threaded through that (for me!) impossibly small eye. And I have seen the results—lovely tablecloths, delicate pictures for framing, lovingly created designs to transform the ordinary into the extraordinary.

The transformation that was taking place, however, wasn't simply about tablecloths. It was about ourselves as members of a family in difficulties. By her patient labour and her belief in a better future, my mother pulled us through that period as surely and trustfully as she pulled her embroidery silks through the eye of her needle. She had no guarantees, as she sewed, that there would be a market for her work, and she had no conception, as she placed each stitch, that the whole would become something so much greater than the sum of its constituent threads. As I look back on those long-ago years, I see something of God's transforming love there.

Transformation leads from the place of tears to the place of joy, changing mourning into gladness and the agony of childbirth into the joy of new life. But there is no short cut to transformation. It leads *through* the eye of the needle, not round it, and it demands trust. Sometimes the place of joy seems to elude us for ever, and the eye of the needle seems to be all that there is. The Gethsemane of our pain, and the cold abandonment of Calvary, can tempt us to despair as we struggle to get our life's thread through the narrow 'eye' of our circumstances. We can lose all sight, and all hope, of there ever being a resurrection.

I know now, with the benefit of hindsight, that my mother was trapped in the eye of a needle more sharp and piercing than I, as a child, could ever have guessed. In her own way she was passing through a kind of Calvary, and she made that journey with nothing but love to support her. That was all. That was enough. We came through, but we came through transformed. We learned about patience and resilience. We grew, individually and as a family, from our experience.

It all helps to convince me that God's transformation happens when we embrace the 'eye of the needle', whatever form that may take in our living. We miss out on it every time we try to avoid the constriction of the 'narrow way'. We grow beyond it every time we allow God to draw us through our crisis times on the thread of unconditional love.

'You will have pain, but your pain will turn into joy'

Reflect for a while on any 'narrow ways' through which your own life has led. How did it feel for you at the time, as you passed through the time of difficulty? Can you see any evidence of transformation as a result of your experience? How did it change you?

Lord, please take the broken and separated threads of our own experience, and transform them into the tapestry of your kingdom. Amen

Liberating

About that time King Herod laid violent hands upon some who belonged to the church. He had James, the brother of John, killed with the sword. After he saw that it pleased the Jews, he proceeded to arrest Peter also. (This was during the festival of Unleavened Bread.) When he had seized him, he put him in prison and handed him over to four squads of soldiers to guard him, intending to bring him out to the people after Passover. While Peter was kept in prison, the church prayed fervently to God for him.

The very night before Herod was going to bring him out, Peter, bound with two chains, was sleeping between two soldiers, while guards in front of the door were keeping watch over the prison. Suddenly an angel of the Lord appeared and a light shone in the cell. He tapped Peter on the side and woke him, saying, 'Get up quickly.' And the chains fell off his wrists. The angel said to him, 'Fasten your belt and put on your sandals.' He did so. Then he said to him, 'Wrap your cloak around you and follow me.' Peter went out and followed him; he did not realise that what was happening with the angel's help was real; he thought he was seeing a vision. After they had passed the first and the second guard, they came before the iron gate leading into the city. It opened for them of its own accord, and they went outside and walked along a lane, when suddenly the angel left him. Then Peter came to himself and said, 'Now I am sure that the Lord has sent his angel and rescued me from the hands of Herod and from all that the Jewish people were expecting.'

As soon as he realised this, he went to the house of Mary, the mother of John whose other name was Mark, where many had

gathered and were praying. When he knocked at the outer gate, a maid named Rhoda came to answer. On recognising Peter's voice, she was so overjoyed that, instead of opening the gate, she ran in and announced that Peter was standing at the gate. They said to her, 'You are out of your mind!' But she insisted that it was so. They said, 'It is his angel.' Meanwhile Peter continued knocking; and when they opened the gate, they saw him and were amazed.
ACTS 12:1–16

We have escaped like a bird from the snare of the fowlers; the snare is broken, and we have escaped.
PSALM 124:7

I used to work in a high-rise office block and, like all my colleagues, I needed a magnetic ID card to access any of the offices. One morning I arrived at work, took the lift up to the tenth floor where I was based, and slipped my card through the magnetic reader beside the door. Nothing happened! I tried again, and again, only to be greeted by an unblinking red light that, for me, said that either the whole system had seized up or there was something amiss with my own card. Either way, there seemed to be no way of getting to my desk. I began to wonder whether to go home again, or settle myself out there in the lobby for the day. But by way of one last desperate effort, I waved frantically to attract the attention of my colleagues who were getting on with their work the other side of the closed door, apparently unconcerned about my predicament or the vagaries of the security system.

Eventually one of them noticed me, came ambling across to the door, which he nonchalantly opened, and greeted me with the question, 'What's your problem, Margaret? The door's open. All you needed to do was turn the handle and come in!'

I discovered that the security locking system had failed that day, and all the access doors in the building were behaving like normal doors for once, instead of like portals to Fort Knox. I felt every kind of a fool as I walked to my desk, greeted by the friendly laughter of my workmates.

So I can feel for poor Rhoda! There they all are, praying fervently for Peter's release from captivity, but when the man actually arrives and knocks at the door, no one can believe the evidence of their eyes. So they leave him standing there while they try to rationalise this unexpected turn of events. 'You must be seeing things,' they tell Rhoda. 'It must be some kind of apparition.'

Why is the obvious so difficult to take on board? Why wasn't my first thought to assume that the door was open until proved otherwise? Why didn't Rhoda let Peter in and believe in his liberation?

God must get so frustrated at our obtuseness and our inability to let God *be* God. Just as I tried to place the misbehaving door into the only category I knew—which was 'locked'—so these first Christians placed God's liberating miracle into the only category they understood, which was 'impossible'. As long as we insist on remaining in our closed boxes of limited understanding, God's liberating love can be blocked. And as long as we insist on remaining in cages that our own mindsets have manufactured, we won't be able to walk free into God's tomorrow.

'The chains fell off his wrists'

God's freedom can be so much easier than we dare imagine, if we let its power free us from the mindset that convinces us we are captive in particular situations.

Is there any situation in your own life where you feel imprisoned? If so, talk it through with the Lord in your prayer, and ask him to open your eyes and your mind to 'try the door'. It may open more readily than you think. Sometimes just a slight shift of attitude or expectation can move an intractable situation forward, so that new growth can begin.

Lord, nothing so entraps us as our own conviction that we are prisoners. Please give us the courage and the confidence to 'try the doors' of our life's prisons, and the wisdom to shift our thinking just enough to let a little light into our own places of darkness.

Amen